Memoirs of a Runaway

A Story of Hope

Written by Michael Kennon
and Based on a True Story

Michael Kennon

Memoirs of a Runaway:
A Story of Hope
All Rights Reserved.
Copyright 2010 Michael Kennon

Cover Photo 2010 Michael Kennon.
All rights reserved – used with permission.

Contact the author and check for additional projects through this site; http://www.memoirsofarunaway.com

dedications

to my angels-
mom, thanks for being the one constant in my life,
mark, thanks for being my best friend.
cassidy, besides god, you were my hope and reason for being,
my loving wife, your love and continued devotion
gives me courage and strength,
i love my life with you.

… Michael Kennon

acknowledgements

debra markowitz,
this book would not be possible without you.
henik host-madsen for posing on the cover.
to all in this book: it is with great honor and gratitude
that i tell this story. my life would not have been the same
without you.

Prelude

Thought maybe I should be getting back on the road again, but for different reasons this time. For the first time, I am no longer running or hiding, but just wanting to get some fresh air and take a little break from work. Or rather change where I do what I do and make it mean so much more. There's a lot that keeps me here now, but that wasn't always the case.

At 45, my memory isn't what it once was; brain cells left at too many clubs and with too many nights of indulgence, but remnants of the feelings still remain. I can't fathom how I survived and know that someone was looking after me. I find myself on the verge of my 46th birthday, wanting to document. Wanting to put the pieces together to help myself and to maybe help someone else. Surely, I could not have lived through what I did without a concrete reason for it happening. And even with things being as good as they are, I still screw up.

Chapter 1

2005

On Sue's 40th birthday I asked her what she wanted. Her only request was tickets for a Cubs' game. That sounded great, as I am also a fan. Distractions and becoming preoccupied seemed to consume me each day. I was trying to confront issues of why I was finding it impossible to move on. I was getting tired of glorifying my past and telling people the story of my life. I was still avoiding the issues that kept me from being my best. Around Memorial Day, two weeks before Sue's birthday, I still had not gotten the tickets. I tucked my tail between my legs, went up to her and again asked, "So, what else do you want to do for your birthday?"

I could see the look of frustration on her face as she answered, "You waited until two weeks before the game to get tickets?"

I knew I was in trouble with her and was even more aware that I was getting too comfortable in this relationship and not giving it the attention it deserved. I didn't want to be a disappointment to someone again. Sue and I had been together for almost five years and in my history of relationships, by now I would have done something to sabotage things. But I was very happy in our relationship and I knew the time had come to deal with my mountain or God.

I called some friends that might have been able to get last minute tickets to the game, but they all came up empty. Scanning through websites to see if anyone had turned in tickets in the last minute was a bust. Although not giving up, I faced up to Sue that I had blown it.

I had learned to pray to God for many things so I figured that asking for Cubs tickets might seem a bit trivial, but it wasn't just the tickets that were riding on this. First, I argued with myself trying to avoid feeling guilty. Even Sue was not that mad, just disappointed. Something in me knew that I should not give up. So I spoke to God as plainly as I'm writing this on my laptop. "Lord, I know that I am not doing my best right now. I know that I just think about myself all the time. It's just a defense mechanism when I say that I've had such a hard time in my life that I don't know how to give to others anymore. I want to think of others and be able to give more, but I just don't know how to tear down this wall that I've built up inside of me. I'm tired of asking for things for myself all the time; I want to be a giver. I promise if you get Cubs tickets for me, I'll start to work on my past and try not to be so selfish anymore." I had a million conversations with God by now, so I just talked to Him like He was one of my buddies. By this time in my life, I had suspicions that without God or a Guardian Angel there was no way I would have made it this far. I did not know God, I did not know I could trust God, I wasn't even sure if I believed in God, but I knew that I was either very lucky or someone was watching over me.

What I did know was that the next day was Sue's birthday. Sitting in front of my computer on Saturday evening trying to think of what I was going to do to make up for this, I thought that maybe I would take her dancing. That would be a miracle in itself for me. Maybe a fancy restaurant would work. I went to Cubs.com, and I stared at the site and thought, "Wow, there are two tickets for sale, but I know this has to be wrong." I had done this before when they say tickets are available, but you go to buy them and they're gone already. I looked a little closer to see that they were on the third base line just five rows up from the Cub's dugout. Even if they are real, I figured, they were going to cost at least $1,000. So I checked. Hmm, I thought. It says they're on sale for the regular price. I knew it was just a teaser, but I figured that I would try to catch the carrot for the heck of it. I whipped out my credit card and hit the Accept button. "Congratulations on your purchase," the website replied. "Your confirmation has been sent." Staring at the screen, I thought to myself, "No way!"

Sue and I took the train down to Wrigley Field. We left with enough time so we could arrive at least two hours early because we were so excited and because we wanted to beat the crowd. As we walked inside, a man with a clipboard walked up to me and said, "Would you like to participate in a promotional deal with the Cubs?"

"I'd love to," I replied, "but this is Sue's birthday, and this would be a thrill for her."

"That's great," the man said. "Well, let me explain what this is about. We'll take you up to the actual room where we take the players to have them sign contracts and have you sign some release forms. Then we'll pick a position for you and take you down to the field. You'll go out onto the field and take that player's position. Then the player will take the field, come out to you, sign a baseball for you and then you'll come back off the field."

As I looked at him, listening intently, my gaze turned to Sue who looked like an excited 12-year-old on her 40th birthday. She looked as giddy as a schoolgirl. I took tons of pictures and even got one of her name on the scoreboard taking the catcher's position. Later that day, Joe Girardi got the winning hit. He was the catcher that Sue got to stand with on Wrigley Field. He's the one that signed her baseball and even thanked her for coming out when we knew that it was a miracle that we were even there.

After that day, I started reflecting more on the past and thought, luck or not, I had better not take a chance that God does not exist and maybe I should stop ignoring him. I started contemplating what I was supposed to do, wondering whether I should talk to Him like he was my own personal psychiatrist or tell someone else about my past so that it could help me sort some things out.

Already having gone to counselors, psychiatrists and men of the cloth before and explaining, telling and confessing everything, I wondered what it would take to finally work things out. I've had one relationship after another, and I was aware that I had used them in order to find myself. Sometimes I latched on so tightly that I suffocated the ones I loved or didn't give them the time of day when they needed me most. Basically, I ended up hurting everyone I had ever been involved with.

I had thought about blocking things out and ignoring everything that had happened. That's what a lot of people do and what I had always done. Maybe I needed to help someone else so that I could help myself. Maybe that's why things never got permanently resolved. It seemed like it had been so long since I'd really laughed or felt like the world was not coming to an end. I wanted to feel free again.

So, reflecting on Sue's birthday and the miracle of the Cub's tickets, remembering all I had been through to get where I am but knowing I've still not quite made it, I bring myself back to the present moment.

I am filled with so much anticipation that it feels like I cannot breathe. As much as I have moved on, something still needs to be done; I feel it, I live it. Maybe I'm supposed to do more than just *get over it*. So I sit here on the deck of our new home with my laptop perched on the picnic table and stare out at the sunset as it glistens over the lake. Though life seems perfect, maybe I need to go back and tell you about when it wasn't always so…

Chapter 2
1971

My mom called me Michael, sometimes Mike. The kids called me Mikie. They would taunt me. Compared me to the kid in the commercial that didn't like anything. Or they'd call me, Michael, Michael Motorcycle, and I'd say, "Yeah, he's cool, I want to be like him," or "yeah, that's me." I didn't have hard feelings though. I don't think it was reverse psychology, it was just who I was.

It was a good life in Crystal Lake, Illinois. There were a lot of kids in the neighborhood, and Dad put a basketball hoop up in the driveway for all of us, though Mark, my brother, was too young and small to play. He was only four, and at the time, small for his age.

I remember staying up late at night and reading *Peanuts*. Snoopy was the coolest, but I felt like Charlie Brown. Like him, I wanted to have a lot of friends and be around people, but it often felt like I could do nothing right. It didn't help that I was hyperactive from ages five to fourteen and had to be on Ritalin during that time period. I remember a story my mom told me about a neighbor wanting to come over to escape from her cat who was in heat. As they sat there sipping lemonade, they watched me swinging like Tarzan from tree to tree. Like most children, I didn't know the meaning of mortality, but being hyperactive as well made me consistent in my escapades. The neighbor stayed for half an hour and finally said, "Jan, I appreciate the break, but your son is surely going to drive me crazy if I have to watch him much longer. I'll take my chances with the cat." And off she went.

But life seemed pretty good regardless of my quirks. I was a capable athlete; several kids on the block and I played running games, and I was one of the fastest in the group. Being a creative, resourceful young man, I was always building things or taking them apart. Some of the things I created were a bit on the mischievous side. Being younger, Mark would go along with a lot of my schemes. I came up with the idea of calling random people and telling them that I was a lost little boy who was scared out of my wits and waiting at a convenience store. Ten out of twelve of these unsuspecting participants would go to the 7-11 to try and help me. I'm not proud of that now, but I see how it was the basis for what I was to become – good and bad – in the years ahead. My aunt used to tell me that I could sell ice to the Eskimos; a great trait when used in the correct way, but as it came to be known, I didn't always use it properly.

When the summers came, I would spend them at my grandmother's house in the Ozarks. Dolly was my Dad's mom, and she was loved by everyone. For as long as I could remember, my grandmother had snow white hair, though she always kept it shoulder length and stylish. She never denied her age and always took pride in her appearance. She was short and round and seemed like a grandmother everyone could love with her great disposition and genuine smile. Grandma Dolly loved bird watching and loved people even more. When she would come back from the many walks she enjoyed, she would tell me about which birds she saw. I learned to water-ski at Grandma Dolly's when I was seven. Another summer, I built a sailboat out of Styrofoam and lumber that I had found. Grandma always had a kind word and took great interest in my dreams and fantasies.

Neighbors and friends would come down to their cabins almost every weekend in this resort area. The friends that vacationed next to my grandmother had a daughter named Candy. She was a pretty girl with long, straight black hair all the way down her back. She was always a little mischievous, and we would spend a great deal of time together talking, sharing and doing impish things. Candy was my first experience with puppy love. Although I was a busybody, I was a pretty good kid. I saw Candy on and off from age 7 until I was about 13. She was the first girl I kissed. When she gave me a puff off of her cigarette, I acted like I had done it before. I was afraid of getting caught, but I did not let on. I was infatuated with Candy, and we would spend hours together kissing under the dock. Summers were paradise for me in the Ozarks.

Besides the A.D.H.D., I would also discover that I had food, chemical and inhalant allergies. I was especially allergic to dust, mold and house mites. I had a horrible diet, which didn't help things, and my energy level was off the charts. But still I remember a great childhood. My mom, Jan, was a successful RN, wife and mother. She and my father had a wonderful relationship. I assumed it would always remain that way and that, one day, I would have a relationship like them.

I later learned that my dad was hyperactive too. What I remember of him was that he was a great writer, published author and excelled in every task he took on. Mom used to say that he had a real knack for making the reader feel that he was talking directly to them. And I do remember the newscasts from the local radio stations. When I played baseball, I would imagine my dad narrating the games and being so proud when I'd strike someone out or pitch a no-hitter. Dad was the Vice President of Public Relations for Union Oil, a high position for a large company, where he got to use his people and writing skills.

Dad was always active. He smoked three packs of cigarettes a day, but 2-1/2 of them sat in the ashtray burning as he worked on one project or another.

He loved to travel, and I still have great photos from vacations we took at Bush Gardens, the Ozarks to see his mom, and Vandalia to see my aunt on my mother's side. I think my love of traveling was fostered by the family trips we would take and the happiness we shared at each adventure.

My dad got sick when I was 10. He was sick for months with a brain tumor. It wasn't easy to watch your hero wither away, but as a child, you always hope for the best. Sometimes though, there is no denying the truth. As I was sent off to spend an entire afternoon with my Uncle Eddie, I waved goodbye to my dad. He did not look well, but I tried to shake it out of my mind. This was one of the very few memories I have of spending any significant time alone with my uncle. But even though we had fun, I felt anxious. As my uncle dropped me off, my mom came up to me and said that we needed to talk. My heart sank as I knew what would follow. My dad had passed away. Dead at the age of 43. The feelings were both intense sadness but also relief that he didn't suffer anymore. Through the tears I began remembering the good times. My favorite was going to the carnival with my dad and having him slip me $10 while telling me, "Don't tell your mother." We would share a knowing wink, and I would run off to the rides and arcade. We lived on a dead-end street, and sometimes Dad would let me sit on his lap and steer the car around the end.

The papers made a big deal out of Dad dying. "Ex-Newsman Dies at 43. Leslie G. Kennon, Was PR Executive." The clipping went on to talk about Dad's accomplishments. It's one of the few clippings I have from my dad. Unfortunately, it also happened to be his obituary. Somehow, the columns he wrote had disappeared.

When he died, I blamed him for leaving us, and I blamed God for taking him away. I would dream about him returning to us and would feel loved and encouraged as if he were watching over me – but I wanted more. In the early sun, I realized it was just a dream and while I'd like to believe he visited me, I was angry that it was not real.

When I thought of my father, I thought of love and of success. I wanted to be an accomplished man like my father. I always knew I would be and although I didn't know at what, I felt like it was written in the stars. While I would have those visions and feel hope, the other side of me felt alone and abandoned. Because while dreams are nice, I knew my father was not coming back and that my mother, my brother and I were now on our own.

Chapter 3

The years after Dad's death, we did the best we could to survive the trauma. Mom was always busy, and I was a busy body. Mom was very much in love with my father, and it was apparent that there was a huge hole in her life. She kept up a strong front, but you could see that she was missing a part of her heart.

I kept myself occupied by preoccupying my brother, Mark. I'd make up games, the sillier the better. One of them involved Mark picking out different color crayons and handing them to me. I would make up a character to represent each color and find activities to go along with them. An orange crayon would mean that I turned into "Orange Bed," a character that read him bedtime stories. A red crayon meant that I would turn into "Underweary Hairy Monster" and would chase Mark all around the house threatening to get him. I know that I was a handful for my mother, but she was happy that I took Mark's mind off things for the moment. Dad had been the disciplinarian, and since his death, Mom became even more lenient instead of reprimanding us. She knew I didn't mean any real harm, so I could roam free in my mischief.

Cindy was a family friend who spent quite a bit of time over at our house after Dad died. She was trying to talk to Mom, but a loud sound she'd assumed was me jumping from bed to bed began distracting her. "Michael Kennon, what are you doing now?! Fun is fun, but you're plain wearing on my nerves, young man," she shouted up the stairs. It turned out that we'd had a small earthquake in Illinois, but generally, even a small earthquake could not outdo Michael Kennon at his best.

Mom was used to the chaos I created, but I suppose that happens in a lot in families that lose a parent or where divorce tears things apart. And I'm also sure that kids, as smart as they are, go in for the kill once they figure out they can get away with it.

My brother, Mark, was a terrible asthmatic and seemed to get worse after Dad's death. I felt these games I made up would help take the stress off of Mark's loss. I think Mom was secretly glad that I cheered him up at all, no matter what in the house might get damaged in the process.

The allergies I had would intensify my moods. Reactions I would have included moodiness, rebellion, crabbiness and I would sometimes become just downright difficult to deal with.

It was about two years after Dad's death when mom started dating again. She got involved with singles groups, playing bridge, and, thankfully, she had a tremendous support group. But I was worried about us and how we were going to get by. Even at that early age, I knew my Mom had become accustomed to a certain lifestyle. I knew that things were not going to be the same without my father around. I became protective and thought about money all the time. As long as I kept busy I would be okay, but I continued to peer at it, think about it, and it made me nervous. I was young, but I felt that my mother was materialistic. Our family had always been fairly affluent in the past, to the point of being pretentious. I was never really aware of our financial situation and felt we were just getting by. I didn't think my mother's career could support this beautiful house my father had just bought before he died. And I did not know if he had left her money to live on. I knew it was the parents' job to protect their kids from the realities of impending financial doom, but I just couldn't get comfortable and dwelled on it too much.

Chapter 4
1973

Not long after Mom started dating, she met Don. At this time in my life, I was getting taller and growing my light brown hair longer. Mom was still in great shape; in fact she modeled until she was 39. So here was Don. The first one we met, the first one it seemed that my mother was serious with. I wanted my mother to be happy, and I didn't at all think this would be serious, at first. Mom met Don through acquaintances at Union Oil, my dad's old company and where Don worked. One of my first memories of Don occurred when Mark and I were camping in the living room and the zipper on my sleeping bag got stuck. Don came over and fixed it for me, and I found that significant at that time. He was an alright guy. Don seemed to have a desire for love and a tremendous ability to succeed at almost anything he did. I saw him as a man who was witty, competent, confident and quite capable of achieving great things.

As I was very close to my mother, I asked her if she loved Don. She said, "Not the same way I loved your dad, but I care about him and think he'll be a good role model."

They planned a large wedding at our house. Our family friend, Cindy, helped with the wedding invitations. Mom and Don married, and he moved into our house in

Crystal Lake, Illinois. We were all getting settled and life was beginning to return to some sort of normalcy. Don was a graduate of one of the top universities and also worked as a bigwig for Union Oil. He was 15 years older than Mom, but I was impressed with his achievements and abilities. He was a big man who was in peak physical condition and was always respectful around my mother and other people.

Sailing was one of the activities we enjoyed. Don had a Snipe and also bought a Sunfish that I sailed all the time when I was 12. I could swim like a fish, and I loved the water. One time I took Mark, who was 7 years old, sailing. It was a beautiful day when we left, and we had not a care in the world. At one point, I turned to look behind me, and I saw a storm coming in. I tried to get back to shore, but the storm came in quickly, and I couldn't outrun it. The Sunfish was overturned, spilling Mark and me into the lake. I was able to find Mark under the water and pull him up. Pure adrenaline and urgent prayers allowed me to hold onto Mark until another boat could rescue us and bring us in. I had nightmares about that incident for years although Mark himself did not seem to be traumatized. He always knew that I would be there to save him. He also liked being a celebrity after having the local paper write about it. I still do love the water to this day. Mom was also very enthusiastic about sailing and did not take a backseat to Don when they were on the water. She was a very hands-on person on the boat. They had friends that took them on sailing adventures to Florida and the Caribbean. My uncle even lived on a sailboat in Hawaii. Those were good times. Carefree, as if some of the pain of my father's death subsided, and we could relax for a while.

Mom belonged to the First Congregational Church and when she and Don began dating, we went as a family. Don and Mom also started traveling, and Don took her to visit his relatives in Amsterdam. They also went to Florida and Park City, Utah. We were an active unit. Boating when water was available and skiing when we could get to the slopes; I remain an avid skier. I've done freestyle skiing and also skied some of the toughest slopes.

Besides our family activities, Mom kept busy with her bridge club, tennis, her country club activities, classes, seminars, and of course, us. She was the perfect wife for a high-powered man like Don. Don did a lot of work around the yard as we had an acre of land, sailed constantly, and was brilliant on the piano, which he played every day. He was always building and fixing things around the house. He also bought and drove an old, beat-up orange and white pick-up truck that he used to haul trash from our yard or to buy things for the house. He also purchased a new Blazer for Mom and a new Corvette for himself. That Corvette got stolen at Union Oil in the middle of the day while he was at work one day.

We were busy, we were happy; we had a reprieve from grieving over my dad. I thought that things were going to be okay, but it turns out they were to be far from okay.

Chapter 5

I can't pinpoint the exact moment during which things began to change. Don always had a good sense of humor, but the tone of his comments turned into sarcasm when it came to me. He would use that sarcasm to make light of a situation, but later he started becoming sarcastic constantly.

Don treated my mother well and was attentive to my brother; it soon began to feel as if I were in the way. I knew my hyperactivity could be a challenge to anyone, but Don seemed to take it personally, as if I just would misbehave to defy him. Though no one could replace my father, I had hoped that Don could be a father figure to me. It became clear by my 13th birthday that I was never going to be loved by this man, was never going to be hugged by him, and he had no intention of bonding with me. I was beginning to feel completely inferior to Don.

First, my grades were never good enough. If I offered any dialogue at the dinner table or in front of the television, I was sneered at. Whenever I opened my mouth, if Don was in the room, there would be verbal sarcasm or a grimace from him.

My mother could see what was going on and tried to be extra attentive to me when she could, but my brother's asthma became so bad that she needed to place her focus on him. He was in the hospital quite a bit and was so skinny that you could see all his ribs when he breathed in. I often felt that Mom needed to give Mark all her love because of his illness. I understood that he needed to be pampered, and I didn't feel jealous as I loved him with all my heart and was afraid, at times, that he might die.

Despite understanding what Mark required, my middle name was "needs attention." Caring for me was like taking care of several children at once. I was lying and stealing and was becoming impossible to discipline. Perhaps, I was testing and punishing my mother for her lack of attention.

With Mom tending to Mark's needs, I had to fend for myself much of the time. I would be home by myself quite a bit, and I learned to cook and entertain myself. Rummaging through the house one time, I came upon Don's golf clubs. I brought them outside and started hitting balls into the marsh in back of our house. I put them away when I finished and found other things to do. When a neighborhood friend came calling the following day, I gladly accepted the excuse to leave the house. We hung out for hours and upon returning home, Don grabbed me by the collar and dragged me over to where the golf clubs lay. He picked up a bent club and yelled, "You little son of a bitch; you bent my golf club." Then he struck me with it, knocking me off of my feet. I crouched over waiting for him to hit me again. He didn't, but he instilled in me not only the fear of what he would say to me, but how he could physically hurt me whenever he chose to. I was so afraid of him at that point that I wanted to do exactly as he told me to. I was afraid that if I told my mother, he would strike me again.

Don had asserted his power. He would begin to hover over me and grab me if I said or did anything that did not please him. As frightened as I was of him grabbing me, I became used to it. I became used to the fear. Don felt that I needed to be controlled. While it was true that my mother was very lenient with me, Don went to the extreme to ensure that I was well-behaved according to his standards. My mother did express discomfort when Don would get physical with me. She and my brother became innocent bystanders while this man would push, shove and grab me to help make his point. Mark, being younger, was petrified and did not step in but would gladly stick up for me when "mean old Don" was out of the house. I felt alone during this period—that no one could, or would, help me.

Though I tried to behave in a way that would not upset Don, I was only an adolescent. When I came in late one evening, Don threw me up against the stairs and began to strike me.

"Rules don't apply to you, Mister. Huh? You can do whatever you want? Well, guess what, this is what you're going to meet up with." Don slapped me hard on the side of my head as he continued to raise his voice. I guess he didn't hit me as hard as he could have, or it would have hurt more. Or maybe when you were scared, you just didn't feel anything. The one thing I actually did feel was fear. I instinctively pulled my arms up to protect my head as Don kept slapping me.

My mother did step in that time. When she did, I ran out the door hoping that when I returned things would have quieted down. Don must have listened to my mother, because things got better for a while. Every time my mother would step in, Don would rein his temper in temporarily. Still, there were always episodes.

One time we were arguing so fiercely, my mother threw water on us both to calm us down and break us up.

The hitting was reserved mostly for times when only Don, I and sometimes Mark were around, the sarcasm was constant and free flowing. Whatever the situation, Don had a comment. He would make sarcastic digs, and very creative ones at that. They were thought provoking and said in a hurtful manner. Don would turn any of my failures, no matter how insignificant, into a joke and make me feel incredibly small. He loved to tell jokes while making sure the person, mainly me, knew that I met with his utmost disapproval.

When I got it in my head to heat up milk in the coffeemaker, Don pulled me aside by the collar of my shirt and said, "You're trouble. You can't do anything right. All you do is destroy things and ruin things for this family. Maybe it's time you grew up and left so we could have some peace in this house. It's not like you're wanted." I had to believe my Mom loved me and wanted me to stay. I knew my actions didn't always turn out for the best, but I didn't mean any harm. I started to feel like the black sheep of the family, and it seemed like a cycle I couldn't reverse.

One morning I felt ill and wanted to stay home from school. My mother agreed that I could. Don felt that I should have gone to school, but he did nothing. The next day, however, when my mother said I could stay home again, Don became furious. He grabbed me and threw me down the stairs. I protected myself as best I could and curled up in a ball as he came down the stairs after me. Then he told me that if I couldn't go to school, I shouldn't have anything to do in my room either. He picked me up by my shirt and pushed me into the closet. He told me to stay there, and I did. I was too terrified to move. I decided then that when I got better, I was going to run away.

I fantasized about my journey on the road, but by the time I was well, I put aside my plan to run away. I tried to run away from the situation while remaining at home. I started staying out with all the neighborhood kids as often as possible. Just as often, I tried to stay overnight so I would not have to go home to a place I was now seeing as a prison, with Don as the warden. Anywhere with a pool table suited me. I would go to clubhouses, friend's houses, pool halls and even bars. Pinball machines would suffice as well. While hanging out with my friends, I smoked and bought cigarettes regularly. I used whatever tactics I could to take myself mentally out of my house of horrors.

My reprieve was going to Grandma Dolly's for the summer. I did a lot of thinking while I was there. I tried to figure out how I could become a man so that I could better take care of myself and not remain victim to Don's domination. I would sit at the lake for hours with my overactive imagination and try to think myself out of the situation. It was unlikely that a 13-year-old could support himself, however I had the confidence that I would be able to. I did a lot of fishing at Grandma Dolly's, and on some starlit nights I would listen to WLS, a radio station almost 600 miles away. Grandma and I would talk for hours. I couldn't share what was happening at home, but I sensed she knew things were difficult for me. She extended me every kindness and display of love, and I felt as if I finally belonged somewhere. But I also knew that I had to return home in the fall. As the end of summer neared, I grew uneasy with the knowledge of the war zone that remained at my home.

When Don and Mom picked me up, I prayed that things would somehow get better, though I didn't hold out much hope. And once back home at Crystal Lake, I fell back into the patterns I had set before I went to the Ozarks. I stayed out as often as possible, and when Don gave me grief, I started running away. One of the first places I went was a music store where they had pinball machines. I would play for hours and got so good that I would get free credits and play most of the night for little money. When the store closed, I did not know where to go so I retreated home.

By 14 years old, I started rebelling. I did not hang out with the neighborhood kids as much, so it felt like I did not have many friends. One day in my freshman year, I went to "smoker's corner" at Crystal Lake High School. One of the girls there offered me a smoke, and I knew that it was not an ordinary cigarette. I accepted the hit, and it seemed that overnight I had a whole new group of friends. As desperate as I was for attention, even then I realized that when I had drugs, I had friends. In order to keep those "friends," I started carrying pot, smoking pot and dealing to support my newfound form of recreation. My new hobby served two purposes – it made sure I was not alone, while also allowing me to escape the reality I lived on a daily basis. As Mark and I got older, Don and Mom started leaving us home alone more. This paved the way for me to start having parties at the house.

I had a stocky build at this time, and started growing my hair longer. My emotions were a whirlwind. I was confident one moment and an emotional wreck the next. I could appear to be a mature man walking into a bar and buying a drink, but the next day I might be climbing a tree just because it was there. I know that a lot of these feelings of ups and downs are part of being a teenager and an adolescent, but being hyperactive and doing daily battle with Don made the highs higher and the lows debilitating.

At 14, I applied for a job at an assembly plant and told them that I was 16. I got the job and used my money to buy pot. I borrowed friends' motorcycles and would ride them over Crystal Lake when it was frozen, through cornfields in the summertime or about anywhere I wouldn't get caught. Whether dangerous or not, I never paid it any thought. I was caught by the same cop while riding through the cornfield on the way home from work. After catching me three days in a row, he searched me, found pot on me and confiscated my friend's bike. I was arrested and put on probation.

Things between my stepfather and me deteriorated to the point where there were no civil times between us. This challenged my mother so much that she started overlooking the fact that I was not coming home on a regular basis. When I did go to school, I did poorly. Most times, I would just skip. The regular calls from the school with regards to my cutting and grades were the last straw for my mother at that time.

She decided that it might do me good to go back and stay with Grandma Dolly. I jumped at the chance. I was enrolled in Reed Springs High School in Missouri and quickly tried to fit in. I was very flattered when a much older girl started talking with me and asking questions. Katie asked me to come to a party at her house, and I was thrilled to be accepted so quickly. Grandma Dolly was happy that I had found a friend. After school I showered, changed and took my bike to Katie's house. At first I thought I was early, but it didn't take long for me to realize that the two of us and another couple were the only people expected to be there. Katie and I got high with the other couple, who were a bit older, then Katie took me by the hand, and we left the house. We walked over to an old, abandoned car where we had sex in the back seat. She was my first, and while I thought I would finally have someone to love me, apparently Katie did not equate sex with love. That was probably one of the few areas I was naïve in; sex and love.

I never did go out with Katie again but found my way to a much older group. The place to be, it turned out, was at a mobile home owned by Kit and Chuck. Their mobile home was on several acres in the Ozarks, and it turned out that they were a couple of the biggest drug dealers around. They had constant parties, and drugs were always available for purchase or sampling. Anyone could come by, and if they got too high to leave, they could just crash on the couch or the floor. I spent many nights wasted out of my mind and woke up with my face buried in their orange shag carpet with the taste of stale cigarettes, pot and warm beer in my mouth. I met a lot of women through Kit and Chuck's parties. Even though I wasn't old enough to drive, I hooked up with a girl who let me drive her all over in her 1968 Cobra 2. Dee was only 16, and her father was a political figure in the area. The father and her brother supped up the car, which was left at her brother's house. Her brother let me drive the car assuming that I had my driver's license. Dee and I traveled from one end of the Ozarks to the other, and she often let me use her car to drag race across the Kimberling City Bridge. One time, the police caught me speeding across the bridge, but I punched it and tried to flee. The chase went on for what seemed to be an eternity until another car pulled out in front of us and I was able to out maneuver the policeman and got away.

My love for my cars and my innate ability to drive effectively and accurately provided a sideline for me to earn money. At only 14, I learned how I could race cars, sell more drugs and have a constant supply of about anything I wanted.

Grandma Dolly never made mention of my activities, and I was always respectful to her when I was home. She worked at the Silver Dollar City amusement park, and she got me my first job there. My friend, Dennis, from school worked there as well. We would make a game out of seeing how many girls we could pick up and take on rides. One girl I met, Desiree, was there with the Christian Choir Group from Montana. She was 16, and I was just 14. Desiree was a sweet girl with long brunette hair parted down the middle. She was naïve and a virgin to just about everything. She said she had never even been on a 'car date' before, and so I told her that I would take her on one.

After spending the entire day together, we did not want to part. Dennis had picked up her friend, Carol, and seemed to hit it off as well. I made plans with Desiree to pick her and Carol up after everyone in their group fell asleep. Dennis and I drove to their hotel and waited outside. We brought beer with us, and we waited late into the night for Desiree and Carol to come outside. About 3:00 am, the girls came scurrying out of the hotel with hushed giggles being shared between them.

Desiree jumped into the back seat with me, while Carol scooted in beside Dennis. "Go, just go," Desiree ordered in a frantic, yet muffled tone. We found a clearing in a wooded area, just concealed enough to keep the car hidden. We drank and kissed until it became light out. Dennis brought Carol back so that she could make the 10 am bus trip back to Montana. Desiree stayed with me, and we curled up on a blanket we'd taken from Dennis's car. We woke up in each other's arms. No matter how understanding Grandma Dolly might be, I did not think she would take kindly to my moving a 16-year-old girl into the house. One of my friends wanted to help us and sold me his 1964 Oldsmobile for $50. The car was worth more than that, but whatever we were going to do, we were going to have to make due with the $36 we had left.

Desiree and I were quite excited about heading towards Los Angeles. We went to churches to ask for money, but most the time they would only offer gas and food vouchers. When they could not help us, they would send us somewhere to eat. When we got hot and sticky, we would wash up in the restrooms of the churches and missionaries. We mostly slept in the car. Though tired, we looked forward to arriving in Los Angeles. We would both find jobs and get a little place where we could settle down. Quite a dream for a 14-year-old and a 16-year old, but it was cut short when we visited a church for assistance. Desiree asked if she could use the phone to call her friend in Montana to let her parents know she was okay. The church assistant agreed that Desiree could use the phone. She said that someone would be with us shortly and asked us to put our names on a sign-in sheet on the desk. She walked out of the room as Desiree called Carol. I watched her face with concern as her friend spoke to her. Desiree hung up the phone, nudged me and said, "We need to get out of here." Carol told her that her parents had the police put an APB out on her. We ran from the church, and I drove away as quickly as I could. Our excitement turned to discomfort as we tried to go as far as we could on very little gas. We managed to get through another two towns before we stopped at a shopping center and tried to beg for food and gas money. I handled one side of the center and Desiree went by the other. We managed to panhandle $12, enough to split a burger and put gas in the tank.

"What are we going to do?" pleaded Desiree.

"We'll be alright, baby. When we get to Los Angeles, we'll be able to make our way. Like we said, we'll get jobs. We'll have each other."

"I'm starting to feel like we're not going to make it there. I'm scared, Mike. What if we get caught? What are the police going to do to me?"

I tried to not show the fear that I also felt. I tried to feign confidence, but I was terrified. Scared of getting caught and afraid to be alone again.

We managed to make it through to Kingman, Arizona before the water pump went on the Oldsmobile. Desiree cried and ranted. She had had enough. This was no longer fun for her, and she wanted to go home. She called her parents collect and made arrangements for them to wire her money so that she could take a Greyhound bus home. She was relieved that her parents were happy to hear from her and that there was no screaming or threats. They just wanted her safe and sound.

We made the arrangements and spent one last night in the car. We made love in the back seat, and Desiree promised that she would always remember me. As I saw her off on the Greyhound bus, I smiled and waved goodbye to her.

Despair set in. I had nothing to my name, and since I had pushed everyone away, I felt that no one cared for me. My moods continued to be erratic—fantasizing about becoming famous but flirting with the idea of suicide. I didn't know where to turn. It was tiring to keep looking over my shoulder, as I was truant. The big man that I was became a child, time and time again. I could hitchhike across the county, but I often wanted someone to take care of me.

I did not have any money to fix the car so I left it there and decided to hitchhike to Los Angeles. It would be easier, and quicker, alone. Two men in a van picked me up and told me that they were doing drive-aways. People who were moving or were going on vacation might fly or take a moving van to their destination, and in turn, would pay someone to drive their car for them. They hooked me up with contacts for drive-aways, and I figured I could drive one car to Portland, Oregon and then another to Los Angeles. So now I had a way to get to somewhere. I had no idea what I was going to do next, but I was gleaming with confidence and would happily tell the people that I ran into, "I'm going to be rich by the age of 22."

Chapter 6

While drive-aways took me to a physical destination, I was at a loss for how to support myself. I lived in my car and again hit up churches for money to buy food. I almost made it a challenge to see how much money I could get from churches. I continued to do this until I acquired a conscience some time later and was able to get food vouchers. I went every where I could think of looking for work; fast food restaurants, temporary agencies, labor jobs, but not one would hire me because I was only 14. Day after day I hit the street looking for work until I noticed some young men unloading a truck. I spoke to one of the drivers, and he hired me as a lumper to move furniture. We traveled around the Los Angeles area for several months, and while I liked the idea of driving a truck, moving furniture was tiring and physically exhausting.

There was still plenty of time to reach my goal of being rich by age 22, but this wasn't going to be the way to do it. Without being able to secure a job, I had little chance of progressing. I gathered up my belongings and decided to go back to Illinois to finish school.

In 1976, a couple of months before my 15th birthday, I stuck my thumb out and headed back home. I didn't mind hitchhiking, and there always seemed to be a ride available. Everyone had their own stories, and I enjoyed listening and learning from them. Thinking back on those days from the present, I shudder to think about all the

Memoirs of a Runaway

things that could have happened to me. Hitchhiking in the present time is akin to Russian roulette, but I didn't take anyone's advice back then.

An 18-wheeler pulled over to pick me up, and I climbed on in. "How far are you going?" asked a very large black man. I told him I was going back home to Illinois and he said, "Well, I'm not supposed to take riders, but if you'll duck into the sleeper at the scales, I'll take you as far as I can." His name was Ken, and we talked non-stop for hours. I told him about my stepfather and the reason I was out here. I also told him about my plans to return to a normal life. Ken bought me dinner at a truck stop and told me that he had been married a short time and that he and his wife were expecting their first child. It was a fast friendship, and when he pulled into a truck stop for the night, he said that if I didn't mind bunking with him, he would take me all the way back to Illinois.

To me it was like sleeping with a brother or a friend, as I had no gay tendencies. Ken, however, saw things another way. The space between us was tight, but he began inching closer to me. At first I thought it was just involuntary movements in his sleep until I felt his hand reach around to my crotch. I was afraid, but I was more afraid of being left out in the middle of nowhere. I told Ken that I really liked him but was not interested in being physical. I was relieved that when I said, "no," he stopped his pursuit. He did not throw me out of his truck, and in the morning, he had another offer.

"You can sit on the doghouse and steer the truck," he offered. I was excited by the chance to drive a truck at 14, and gladly took the driver's seat. "You're doing a great job," Ken said. "If things don't work out at home, why don't you give me a call and I'll teach you how to drive the truck, and secure and tarp the loads?"

"Wow," I expressed. "I will probably take you up on that sometime." If things didn't work out with Don, at least I had somewhere to go.

Chapter 7

My mother was very happy to see me, but I came back with bottled up anger at Don. I was much more defiant. I was difficult to live with and harder to control. Don treated my mother very well and was trying to make things work with me. We went to counseling together and tried doing the family things we had once done before things turned bad between us. Don had purchased a condo in Park City, Utah, and took us skiing. We had fun, but there was an unspoken tension between us. We went to Treasure Island, Florida where we boated and skied on the water. Fun again, but things did not feel real. After having been on my own, I knew that I should finish school and remain with my family, but things were different now.

I played the part as best I could and remained at home for another year. At 16, I was back at Crystal Lake High School and maintaining decent grades. I did not allow my partying to interfere with school, but I did not take great pains to hide it either. I still stayed out with my friends but tried to cause less trouble around the house. On my way home from a friend's house, I cut through a neighbor's yard. A short while later a man was banging and yelling loudly at the front door. My mom opened the door, and man screamed, "You burned down our fort." I had seen the fire on the way home, and I realized that they thought I had set it. Although I was no angel, I was upset that I was being blamed for something I had nothing to do with. The man continued accusing, "If I find a gas can, I'll know that you set it." As he stormed out of the door and started looking around the outside of the house, Mom said to me, "What did you do?" I tried to explain to her that I had not set the fire; I was just in the wrong place at the wrong time. I know she didn't believe me, and how, after so many screw-ups, could I convince her that I was innocent? I learned soon enough that their neighbor was in there smoking and set the fort on fire by accident. I didn't tell anyone, though. The next day at school, a friend of the guy whose fort burned down jumped me. I tried not to fight him. I was trying to defend myself and deflect the situation, but I was called into the office and quickly expelled.

Don did not want to hear about my innocence and, to avoid confrontation, I decided to run away again. Mom tried to make me stay, but I told her that I just would not live with Don. I knew my presence caused tension in the house, and I thought this would be best for all.

I hit the road but did not plan to go far this time. I had made some friends in Pistakee Highlands, Illinois, and met Robert when he picked me up hitchhiking. Robert was renovating a house in Cary, right on the way, and invited me to get high with him. Robert was an intelligent guy who would buy quarter pounds of pot, and we would sit there and smoke till we could not think anymore. When I got to Pistakee, my friends had many more drugs available. I experimented with cocaine, acid and speed. I needed to be part of this group, any group, and would do anything they had available. I began to make a living by dealing drugs. I learned quickly that I could make good money if I wasn't a heavy user. Even with all the drugs I was doing, I could not say I was addicted. I'd seen other dealers deal just to support their own habits, but I did not do that. In fact I rarely, if ever, partied or did drugs by myself. It was more of a social way I found of being accepted. Having a constant supply of drugs meant that I had a constant flow of friends. I would party with everyone, and I felt my life becoming a rollercoaster like the ones back in Silver Dollar City, but without maintenance and headed towards disaster.

My health began deteriorating, and my friends said it sounded as if I would soon cough up a lung. I was tired and ailing, and I called Mom who told me to come home. Cary Grove High School had agreed to accept me, and I was happy to go home and back to school.

Things were not much different at home. We were all trying, though. At the new high school, I quickly hooked up with Kathy. Kathy was trusted to stay home by herself while her parents were away for a few weeks. After one date, I stayed at Kathy's house and did not return to high school. I stayed with her until her uncle found out that I was living there and kicked me out. I knew that it had taken a lot for Mom and Don to get Cary Grove High to accept me, and I could not face them. I did not return home and instead started hitching towards Fox Lake, Illinois. An elderly woman and her son picked me up and said that I could stay with them, if I got a steady job. Desperately wanting to get away from the drug scene, I took a job selling encyclopedias door-to-door. I still had that "selling ice to the Eskimos" thing going for me, so I soon became the second to the top salesperson. I was consumed by reaching the number one slot. I did not let weather deter me and would work late into the night and through the freezing rain. My ambition, coupled with the remnants of my last cough, put me in the hospital with walking pneumonia.

My mother took me home to care for me. I knew that I would not stay, and as I got better, I had already decided that I would not give things a chance. I took off again and went to be with my friends in Pistakee Highlands. My mother called the police many times trying to get me to return home, and while the McHenry Police Department did pick me up several times, I would always run away again. And always when running away, I would find other runaways. All had bad home situations.

I met two young women. Nicki was 14, petite with long black hair, and Helen, 16, who was very tall and was an extremely attractive young woman. Helen had been offered modeling jobs because of her beauty and height. Nicki and I went thru so many experiences, and I was very much in love with her. For a year, we avoided and ran from the police. The courts were so tired of getting calls from Nicki's mother that they actually asked me to get involved with the counselors and the courts because she was already on court supervision, and the next step was to lock her up. I was able to be a mediator and talk her into staying home. However, her mother was a relentless Jehovah Witness and Jesus freak and continued to push her. When Nicki ran away again, I ran with her. The police actually caught us running thru the woods trying to escape them. Still, the courts would not take her and put her back into her mother's custody. Things between Nicki and I became so strained that I began getting closer to Helen. Nicki said I should just stay with Helen because we would not be able to be together. I thought about all we had been through and agreed with Nicki to stay away from each other. When I started going over to Helen's, I had to sneak thru the woods or crouch down in someone's car because Helen and Nicki lived about three blocks away from each other.

Being with Helen was not without stress either. Helen's dad was a security guard who worked the night shift, so her house became the party place in the neighborhood. One night, he came home while we were in bed together. He must have known or thought people were in the house because he had stormed into her bedroom. I narrowly escaped into the closet and had to scurry up my clothes but forgot my shoes. Thankfully, even though I knew he looked right at my shoes, he yelled, "I know you've had a man in this house," and walked out of her room. Helen's father had also been drinking and when I left, I was really scared for Helen as she said he'd been threatening her. That's when I talked to her about moving to her mother's house in Florida. When I called Helen the next day, she said that her father had hurt her bad. I pushed her to call her mother who insisted she move down to Dunedin, Florida. While I saw Helen off, I made plans to hitchhike down to Florida to be with her.

Hitchhiking was second nature to me now. I had had close calls, but I seemed seasoned enough at 16 to avoid getting hurt. I thought it was a sign that the first ride I got on my way to Florida was from a Jaguar limousine. As I got closer to Florida, I got picked up by a man who said he was with the rock band, Supertramp. He told me that someone in his family had died, and he had just picked up this car that was left to him. I thought, perhaps, that these were omens and that when I reached Helen, all would be fine between us. When I reached her house, however, her mother said that she would not allow Helen to see me. She said that Helen was starting a whole new life and that I was not to be a part of it. Helen snuck out to meet me that night, and her mother called the police on me. They picked me up and put me in a group home, but I escaped the next day. I was able to see Helen at her girlfriend's house so that we could be together one last time.

Helen introduced me to her friends, Dave and Cheri, who were both 14. Helen had told her mom she was staying the night at her girlfriends' house, so we all spent the night together, walking and talking, and I was telling them stories of my running away. I didn't mean to glorify this for them because for all the cool things that happened, there was also all the loneliness and despair of being alone. The misery of having to live in your car (or wherever I could stay) and scrounge for your next meal. Eluding the police was stressful, and you were always looking over your shoulder. I guess the other stories I told them made life on the road look like fun. I hadn't meant that. Dave and Cheri were not even supposed to be together, but they decided to go to Cheri's uncle's home in New Mexico. I felt responsible for putting the thought of running away into their heads and became protective of this young couple. I told them that I would go with them, and they were happy about that.

Memoirs of a Runaway

The very first ride we got was from a truck driver, a big burley man named Jack. I did not have a good feeling about this, but I thought that we would get a new ride as soon as we could. Jack pulled into a rest stop a short ways up the road and made a pass at Cheri. We jumped out of the truck and ran until we saw the driver pass us by. The next rides we got were without incident, and we made it as far as Cullman, Alabama where the local police arrested us. Dave's and Cheri's parents had put APBs out on them. They were both sent home to their parents in quick time. I, on the other hand, did not want to go home. Although I was only 16, I told the police I was 18. One of the police officers brought me into a room and showed me a marijuana plant.

"You know what that plant is over there, son?" he asked as he nodded.

"Yes, sir. It's a pot plant," I replied.

"You're in the south here, boy, and we do what we want around here. And you are in big trouble. We could arrest you for harboring fugitives, escorting fugitives across state lines and contributing to the delinquency of minors. You know how long you could be here, boy?"

I was plenty scared. I told them I was only 17, hoping that would be young enough to be considered a minor myself. I did not think that going home would be preferable to this, but it didn't help that they threw me in jail.

There were two men in the cell that looked like rough southern boys. They immediately started harassing me, calling me a "damn Yankee" and we started a shouting match. Then a shoving match erupted as I stood up for myself and the officers came in to break us up. The men were released shortly after, and I was there alone.

Hours ticked by and then turned into days. There was a young woman in the cell next to me who had been there since I arrived. We started talking, and she was as scared as I was. There was a hole in the wall under our beds and we would lay there and talk. We would often touch each other when no one was around. Having her around helped me get through my time there, but still, it started to get to me.

As the days went by, I watched others come and go. I held on for two weeks before I broke down and told the officers that I was only 16 and asked if I could call my folks. My mother answered the phone, and soon after, they escorted me to and watched me get on a Greyhound bus headed toward home.

Chapter 8

It was a long ride home on that Greyhound bus, and you'd think I'd be worried about facing Don after this last ordeal. I guess something in me had changed as I sat in the back of the bus with a bunch of other young people smoking and partying and living a seemingly carefree life.

My mom picked me up, and we started talking as if nothing had happened. When we got home, I walked through the door and Don, a 6'4", 215 pound man who I had never stood up to, hovered over me and started yelling, pushing me, posed to strike at any second. I was a passive person who did not like to start fights, and although I adopted a "the bigger they are, the harder they fall" attitude, it was all for show. I was older, stronger and tired of being harassed by Don. I did not take it this time. I pushed Don through a first-story window in our living room. Don looked stunned and my mother was panicking. She was not taking sides, but I would like to think I saw a look of relief on her face that I finally stood up for myself. That was quickly followed by a look that suggested that she was worried about what would come next. I had thoughts of Don grabbing the gun I had once found in the house. Don just stood up, brushed himself off and walked away. He came back a few minutes later, and without a word, he started taking the broken pieces of glass out of the window frame.

Things actually started to get better between Don and me after that. Even with things calming down in the house, however, I did not want to listen to anyone. I was stubborn and headstrong and used to fending for myself.

I contacted my friend Robert, and he was buying another house in Algonquin, Illinois. He said if I wanted to help him, I could live there rent-free. Robert said he would hook me up with everything I needed and that he was glad for the company. I moved in, and we worked hard and played even harder. Falling into old habits, we drank and smoked way too much. We used to smoke until we couldn't think; now we smoked until we were almost unconscious saying the pot 'increased our senses'.

I'd been through so much, but I always knew I would bounce back. I was shocked one morning waking up with Robert in my bed and realized he had taken advantage of me while I was too stoned to defend myself. I was ashamed and embarrassed. I told Robert how I felt and told him how disgusted I was by what had happened. I said that I would not judge him as long as it never happened again, but our relationship suffered. I was too ashamed to go back home, and too proud to tell anyone. I did not want to go back home either, but I couldn't chance this happening again. I felt that I didn't have a choice.

The new school year was fast approaching and Mother and Don thought they'd try something new with me. They wanted to send me to a private school called Wayland Academy in Beaver Dam, Wisconsin. My Mom and I walked into the registration room, and I noticed a young man who had long hair down the middle of his back, as I did. We hit it off famously, and besides the fact that our birthdays were one day apart, we had much in common. Alex had a dorm room in the basement of the school, which was filled with smoke half the time. Alex would play the drums, and I would try to keep up on the keyboard. Wayland would become a stepping-stone school for all types of drugs. I felt intimidated as if many of the students knew more about drugs and used more drugs than I even knew about. Although I was not ready for sainthood or anything near it, I wanted a change. It was hard for me to make more constructive types of friends, though that is what I wanted at that point in my life. I wanted to be accepted, and the destructive path was all I knew.

I had started doing well with my grades at Wayland, although I was doing speed to stay awake during the day and doing cocaine and smoking pot at night. We would have contests to see who could hold a bong hit the longest, hyperventilate or whatever we could think of to see how high we could get or who would pass out first.

One of my friends and I snuck out to see a Frank Zappa concert, but the school found out and asked that I not come back. I used some of the money meant for school to get a cheap car. When I could not stay at a friend's place, I would sleep in my car.

Alex and I started going to friends places off campus to party, and I started hanging out with this new partying group. By then, with no school work to concentrate on, I was doing all I could to escape reality.

The people I was hanging out with brought me more into cocaine and acid use, and I started to feel like I had nothing to lose. As much as I wanted to have close friendships and still longing for home, I felt that I could only keep these people interested in me by doing the drugs they were doing. I continued to blame Don and God for sticking me in these situations. I did not blame myself or take responsibility for my actions. Though I always enjoyed drugs in the past, I was not controlled by them. Now I found myself becoming addicted. All I wanted to do was get high and struggled to want to change.

During the summer of 1977, I was back in Chicago. Sometimes, I lived at home and other times floating from place to place. I took runs with Ken and sometimes worked and stayed with Robert as well. Most of the time, I was able to find work and almost always got jobs by lying about having more experience than I did. I was learning to become a master manipulator and conned my way in and out of just about anything. Even though I lied about my job experience and age, I was a hard worker and would always give my all to a new job. My inexperience was never discovered, so I felt justified that even though I lied to get the job, it was justified by my performance.

I was still only 16, but almost always had a car even though I did not yet have a legal driver's license. I did obtain the license of man who was 23, and I used that to drive a car and a semi until I had that license stolen some years later.

I felt confident about being able to get, hold and master almost any job I put my mind to, but there was still something I did not have; a family or the will to settle down.

I moved in with a young man named Doug, his wife, Amy, and six year old child. Doug had been into competitive martial arts for over six years and was a six degree black belt. Doug and his family lived in a small farmhouse right in Crystal Lake and I brought all my childhood things, a bed, console stereo, etc and moved into a small apartment they had set up to rent upstairs.

At the time I had also started dating a young lady named Linda, and we all got along well and enjoyed the many many stories Amy told about Doug, their adventures and competitions, as well as listening and sharing my own stories.

Doug and I started spending quite a bit of time together and enjoyed each others company. Doug started taking me under his wing, training and teaching me things he knew. Doug and I were in his living room to start sparring, suddenly, Doug roundhouse kicked me right in the stomach, knocking the wind out of me and dropping me to the floor. Doug said, "Always expect the unexpected."

Linda and I continued to date and after seven months together, I started becoming restless. Linda did not want to have sex until she was married and at 16 I wasn't ready for marriage and had been expressing that to her, but we both wanted to remain friends.

Another young lady from school (as I had once again enrolled in Crystal Lake High School) and I talked about going on a date that weekend. Linda and I still saw each

Michael Kennon

other and talked about the upcoming date and said she'll have to be ok with it as we are now 'just friends'.

At the time I owned a 1965 Chevy Bel-Air and although I went to parties and drove it to school and everywhere, without a driver's license, I did not want to get caught, so would rarely, if ever, have more than three drinks when I was out. Another time I even asked someone to drive me home in my car because I had been getting high.

Since I was straight most the time when I drove, my car could be filled with smoke from pot, cans of beer or alcohol from others riding with me. There always seemed to be and adventure in that car or others. One day after school we were driving through and area of Crystal Lake, called Bull Valley. At the time it was all country roads and I had 5 other people in the car from school when I noticed a Corvette speeding up to pass. The Vet made it around me but I hit the gas and quickly caught up. Everyone in the car urged me to beat him and I went for the pass. Coming around the curve was a fast moving car directly at us. We were forced to leave the road. I saw the road coming back into sight right in front of me and hit the gas again. I jumped back onto the road and caught the Vet again but quickly slowed down as we were all startled. We were all silent in the car for just a second and then we all began to cheer.

The weekend came for my date and while I was out for the day, Linda came over and cried to Doug. She told him she's just not ready to 'let me go' and that I was out on a date with another girl.

Memoirs of a Runaway

Doug came out and found me, but he was enraged. Doug pulled in front of me with his van, punch throw my window and pulled me out of the car and had me up against it, ready to strike. He said, "You better start doing what I taught you or you're dead." I knew if I even flinched, I would be dead. I pleaded with Doug to understand. I explained the circumstances and he let me go saying, "Don't come back for your things".

I went home and told Don what had happened and he said he'd go talk to Doug. When Don came back, he simple said, "Just forget about that stuff".

A few weeks went by and I heard Doug had been getting heavier into drugs. Then a friend told me he had broken into the house of one of his drug dealer friends, beat up the people inside and took the drugs he found. Later, while Doug, his wife and child were at home they went by shooting at the house.

Things were somewhat better between Don and me, but I did not want to stay at home. I was getting restless and went back to Chicago to do some work with Ken. Upon getting paid, I started going to pool halls and practicing my shots over and over. Soon after, I entered a tournament with 136 players. It was double elimination; if you lost twice in a row, you were out. I lost the first game and did not lose again until I got to the last players. I went all the way through to become the top fourth player and won a $300 pool cue.

About that time, I decided I wanted to go someplace warm. Ken was taking a run to Texas, so I decided to tag along with him. On our way down, Ken made another pass at me, and I knew the friendship was over. This man that I respected, admired and was the strongest mentor in my life, had mentally put a bullet in my head. I stayed with him in the cab, but knew the damage was irreparable. By the time we reached Texas, I was desperate to get away from Ken. I saw two girls hitchhiking and asked Ken if he would pick them up.

He said, "No, but I understand if you want to go with them." I jumped at the opportunity.

Anne and Carla told me that they lived in a house not far away and were hitchhiking home. When we got there, there were peyote buttons lying all over the ground with dogs wandering aimlessly around. Anne asked me if I wanted to be with both of them at the same time. It sounded good, and I know it was supposedly every man's fantasy, but it wasn't the life for me. I did want to fit in and also to forget about where my life had taken me. I took one of the peyote buttons but had no idea what the effects would be until it was too late. As the three of us started becoming intimate, I started having the dry heaves and began to hallucinate. Carla told me that the feeling would pass and to just enjoy it. When I could come up for a breather, I began guzzling beer just to feel like I was coming down a little. It only made it worse. When I woke up the next morning, another man who had come over in the middle of the night asked if I wanted a ride back up to the truck stop. I didn't hesitate. One more night like that, I thought, and I'll be dead.

For a change of scenery, I decided to start hitchhiking towards California. I was picked up by a guy who said he was a roadie for one of the bands that was going to be at the California Jam and that he had their drum set. We talked all the way there, and he said he could get me a backstage pass. I was thrilled and once we got there, we started doing mushrooms and smoking joint after joint. I passed out next to one of the huge speakers by the stage. I woke up and wanted to leave because it was so loud that my ears hurt. I could hardly remember watching the concert or meeting anyone because I was so stoned. All I could hear was a ringing in my ears and knew that I suffered permanent damage to my hearing. Life was becoming a constant, loud, confusing haze.

I woke up again in the car of a Hollywood producer. I could not remember how I got there.

"They're good aren't they?" he asked. I had to think about where I was and how I got there. After a minute I remembered someone had asked him to take me home.

"Yeah," I answered, "but I'm not in any condition to enjoy them." I did not know if he meant the band or the drugs, but I played along.

"Where do you live?" he asked.

I told him the story of how I got there and realized that I had been on a bad trip and didn't remember much about getting into the concert, the concert itself, or much else before I somewhat came to my senses in his car. "I was just coming out here to look for work," I replied.

He responded, "Okay, if you want, I have a nice place not too far away from here, and you're welcome to stay for a while if you'd like."

As much as I trusted or didn't trust others, people always seemed to trust me. I must have one of those faces, I thought to myself. I always seemed to get my foot in the door, and I hoped people would continue to trust me and that I would be deserving of it. We arrived at his apartment, and I began to wonder what was in it for the producer. He hadn't asked for anything, and he didn't appear to be on the make. I decided to accept his offer to say at his place and go about looking for work in the morning.

The producer took me to several places, one of which hired me as a laborer. He let me stay for a few more weeks, and we began to talk. He asked that I start calling my mother. He told me that although the living situation at home in Illinois was far from acceptable, it would be much better then me ending up dead somewhere. He continued to show a genuine concern for me.

"Mike, I've worked with a lot of musicians and talented people. I've seen a lot of good men fall in this business. I know you think you've seen a lot, but there are far too many bad influences and situations that you could get into at this age that are much more dangerous than you being in an abusive home."

I took his words to heart and started thinking about the only two people I trusted who did not seem to have a hidden agenda when it came to me—my grandmother and this producer. I began to listen and to think about going home and trying again. I felt that this man must be a guardian angel and that maybe I could start to find my way on the right path.

I said goodbye to my new friend and started hitchhiking back toward Illinois. When I got to Bloomington, Illinois, a man named Eric picked me up.

"Where ya headed?" he asked.

"Not that I'm looking forward to it but back to my parents," I replied.

"If you want, I have a whole big place to myself. There's a bakery next door, and I know they're looking for help," he said.

"I know I should be going home, but I'm really dreading it, and I'm not sure I can face my stepfather." I had resolved to use the advice from the Hollywood producer to make new steps in my life, but I all too soon continued on the course I had set for myself previous to meeting him.

I got the job at the bakery and started making pretty good money. Things were looking up, and I was relieved that I did not have to go home or ask for help. The one bit of advice the producer had given me that I stuck to was calling my mom routinely. I told her almost everything that was going on in my life. The sound of her voice made me happy, and she was comforted by the fact that I was okay.

Settled into my new life, I started playing pool at a local bar after I got off work. We played for hours, and I knew that when I played for money, I would win about 85% of the time. I realized that I might even be able to support myself with my winnings. Shorty was one of the best players, and I knew that he looked forward to playing with me. After a couple of months playing, my pool buddies were getting tired of losing money to me. Four of them forced me out the back of the bar and started uttering threats. I threw the money at them and started getting hysterical. "I thought you guys were my friends," I yelled. "Especially you, Shorty!" Shorty just stood there and smiled. The rest of them didn't say a word; they just picked up my money and grinned at me. Luckily, I was able to slip away without further incident. I told myself I was never going to play pool for money again. I never did use the pool cue I had won in Chicago and it ended up sitting in my mother's closest for the next 16 years.

With my pool days over, I began staying in my apartment after work. A beautiful woman named Betty came into the bakery. It didn't take me long to realize that Betty was the type of woman who used her looks to get almost anything she wanted. Even though I knew that, I was flattered that she wanted me.

Betty soon shared that she was living in a precarious situation with a man who was beating her. She asked if she could move in with me, and I didn't hesitate in responding that it was fine with me. We went back to her apartment and got her waterbed, stereo, her clothes and even steaks from her freezer. The next day, the police showed up at my apartment and arrested me for burglary. The items we removed from Betty's apartment had belonged to her boyfriend. At the same time I was arrested, they had arrested my roommate, Eric, for stealing a motorcycle. The police knew that I lived with Eric and wanted me to tell them more as they suspected, and were correct, that he had stolen cars as well. They threatened me with more jail time if I did not give them information about Eric.

Eric had once picked me up in a brand new convertible. He asked if I was doing anything that day, and as I replied "no," he said we're going up to Rockford Speedway to see Ted Nugent then. On the way he told me

Memoirs of a Runaway

that he had been sneaking through a window at the dealership and taking his pick of cars.

As we drove away from town my heart sank and Eric continued to recklessly speed toward Rockford and I feared for our safety and going to jail. We made it back to Bloomington, and Eric arrogantly parked the car a block away from the dealership and we walked away.

I wasn't about to tell this to the prosecutors however, I kept my mouth shut, but knew that I was in deep trouble.

I was placed in the McLean County Jail, which had a bad reputation for being a tough place. It was the kind of jail where inmates were placed together in one room and the guards looked the other way. I was jumped by a larger, older inmate, but I fought back and managed to fend him off. After that fight, I gained the respect of the other inmates and even befriended the one I had fought with. I knew that keeping up the tough guy persona was key to ensuring my survival in that hellhole. I played chicken with cigarettes as the other inmates watched. As our skin was being scorched by the lit cigarettes, I would not pull away first. I rarely, if ever, lost.

The only call I was allowed to make was one to my mother. She had hired an attorney for me, but I didn't believe they could hold me much longer. The police had arrested me for breaking and entering, but Betty had a key. Her boyfriend did not want to press charges for burglary, but the state did. I had to wait another few weeks for the court date and knew that I had to endure a trial.

I did the best I could to survive day by day. I was in Cullman Jail for 14 days a while ago, but here in McClean County Jail, I felt like I would never get out. I poured my

Michael Kennon

heart out in letters to my mother. Sometimes even Don was addressed in my correspondences. In my letters, I would tell my mom how much I appreciated and loved her. I would try to tell Don how I felt bullied with him around, and didn't he understand that I didn't want to be "bad." I wrote stories and tried to fend off my recurring depression. My letters were sometimes coherent, most times not. There were letters about how I wanted someone to be proud of me, to have respect for me. That I knew it would have to be earned, but I wanted to earn it. Mother wrote me a letter giving me a contract for my return. There would be things I could and couldn't do in order to be able to go home again. Staying clean and sober, getting my GED and a job. All things I was capable of doing. I needed another chance from my family, from society, from the McLean County Jail.

Luckily, when we went to trial, the charges had been dismissed because Betty's boyfriend said that he believed she was behind what had happened, and I was most likely innocent in that matter. After 28 days, I was set free.

It was clear to me that as I progressed on my runaway journey, the incidents that happened to me were becoming graver and more dangerous. I had come to that conclusion before, but I was always easily drawn back into the life I had chosen on the road. I knew that, one day, I would end up in jail long term, or dead. I was old enough to know better at this point. I was no longer a 14-year-old runaway. With my 17th birthday recently behind me, I knew I needed direction. I tried counseling again and did a great deal of soul searching. I finally had to acknowledge that Don was not the cause of my behavioral problems. He may not have dealt with me as he should have, but I caused much of my own pain and made my own choices even though I felt as if I did not have any. I learned in counseling that Don had been beaten as a child if he did not get straight A's, hit with a garden hose if he did not play the piano as well or as often as his father thought he should have or if he skipped a day of practice. Don did the best he could thinking that discipline meant beating your child. When that avenue was taken away from him by my mother, he used sarcasm to try and get me to control my actions. He was not a quitter, and he wasn't about to be challenged by a kid who wasn't even his own. Again, there may be reasons, but there are no excuses. I had started to take some responsibility for my actions.

At this point in my life, Mom had started a new career in environmental medicine involving food and inhalant allergies. I started going to her more for help. She was trying to help me, holistically, to get healthy, hoping that it would help me mentally as well. Even with the progress I was making emotionally, I was not ready to forgive her or God for letting these things happen to me. I wasn't ready to forgive myself either. With all the progress I made, I was still not ready to stop running from life.

I was proud of the knack I had for surviving. I did not know my place in the world, but I knew that I could make money by lying about job experience to get paying jobs, selling drugs or buying and selling cars. It occurred to me that maybe by trying to help others I would learn to help myself.

One of the jobs I talked myself into was working in a hospital for emotionally troubled and retarded children. I felt that if I were able to help someone else, maybe it would, in turn, help me. After going through a psychiatric evaluation, my mom suggested that I see a doctor that did detoxification programs and food and allergy testing. I was enrolled at the hospital for a week to complete the program, and the first thing I did was go through an elimination diet.

I met Mary who was also going through a detox program, and we became our own support group. We replaced our urges for drugs by having sex in the bathroom. One vice substituted for another. I liked Mary a good deal, but I knew that I needed to concentrate on the new job that I would be starting and completing my own detox program. Even though I lied my way in, as always, I intended to do an exceptional job once I was hired. As much as I willingly got involved with Mary, I was discouraged about the actions I kept taking in my life. When she completed her program, she went back to Michigan and I stayed in the hospital for a few more days. I was distraught and without the aid of drugs or sex, I was feeling very alone and vulnerable. To try and ease my pain, I wrote Mary a long letter and told her about the things that had happened to me in my life. When I completed my program, I returned home to try and start fresh. Two days later, Mom took a troubling phone call while I was sitting next to her. It was Mary's mother. After reading my letter, Mary tried to contact me at my mother's house, and someone told her I did not live there.

She was so depressed that she slit her wrist. She survived, but her mother asked that I never contact her again.

Now I was straight and had to think about the consequences of my actions. I not only hurt myself, but I was unintentionally hurting others. I had hoped working at the hospital would help, but I needed more in my life. What I took from the experience of working there was to learn to listen…to others, and to myself. I often believed that if I did nothing, I would be nothing. I realized that I needed to find a place of peace within myself to truly learn who I was. Again, I came to another life-changing conclusion. I needed to give myself a chance to enjoy life and do constructive things instead of always running away from what I was already living. And yet, I still wasn't ready.

Chapter 9

1978

I had been saving my money from my job, and soon I had enough for another car. I drove to the Ozarks to spend some time with Grandma Dolly. My grandmother was always warm and welcoming and had a way of making you feel appreciated and important. Though I had the confidence that I would be financially successful, I needed to feel unconditional love. This was a stressful time for my grandmother, but her generous heart, loving soul and spirit of compassion always shined through. My Uncle Gary, who lived in a small trailer right next to Grandma Dolly's, was a successful magazine editor who had a lot of prestigious friends. Before I had shown up, someone had broken into his trailer and he was stabbed several times. He would recover, but Dolly's husband, my step-grandfather Tony, was taken ill and spent most of his time in bed. I thought about staying elsewhere since things were so difficult for Grandma Dolly at this time, but she insisted that I stay with her until I got on my feet again. She was the only person I have never said no to, and so I stayed.

Memoirs of a Runaway

I took a job selling satellite dishes and quickly rediscovered that talent for sales. I became one of the top salespeople on my shift and the second to the top salesperson for the company. I was proud of the job I was doing and my ability to rise within the company. Determined to make it work, I started panicking when I felt myself slipping. It was like evil was always waiting for me to get just so far away before it started draining the life out of me again. To try to comfort my growing anxiety, I had a brief fling with a lady that I had known from my past there and that just left me more lonely and anxious. To lick my wounds, I went out with my friend, Mark, to our drug dealer friend's house. Mark was getting too high, and they asked us to leave. Mark wanted to go to a bar owned by a friend of his. As I was playing pool, I heard a conversation at the next table.

"Pay me the money you owe me, asshole," a man said to Mark. I did not want a confrontation and tried to intervene.

"Just give him the money, Mark," I said, but Mark refused.

The man he had been playing pool with punched him hard. Before I could step in, several of his friends came over to get me, and I was forced to fight back. It turned into one of those bad movies where everyone is fighting, tables overturning, and pool cues being broken over people's backs. Only this was over $1.00. People were being bloodied and property destroyed over less than the cost to buy a side of French fries. I managed to pick Mark up and get out of the bar just as we heard the sirens. We ran through the woods to escape being caught by the police. I lost Mark, and, in fact, never did see him again. I emerged from the woods after the police had left. I was battered and bloody from running through the woods but was able to get into my car that was parked down the street and drive away. I did not want my grandmother to see me or to know what had happened. Grandma Dolly had enough going on in her life, and I didn't want her to worry about me. I called my mom up, and she agreed that I could come home.

As I was approaching my junior year of high school, one of Don's relatives in Springfield, Oregon said that I could stay with him and finish school at the community college and attend courses to get my high school diploma. In Eugene, Oregon, I attended Lane County College. I was supported by my deceased father's social security, Don's relatives and by Don to live and pay for school.

While at Lane County College, I started up a relationship with a fellow student, Sara. During my relationship with Sara, I learned a lot about becoming a man, learned more about music and starting becoming more responsible. Even with the strides I'd made, however, I did not learn enough. With midterm exams approaching, Sara studied extensively and scored a 92. I had not studied at all but picked up the books a night or two before and scored an 86. Sara was furious. She said this paralleled the way I coasted through life and had everything handed to me. She told me, "You are looking for a mother, not a girlfriend."

I became angry at her, feeling that she did not know all that I went through, but inside I knew she was right. I was still blaming others as I always had, feeling that I should have it easier to compensate for my past hardships. I was lucky and intelligent enough to pass those tests, but I began to wonder whether my luck was running out. I started remembering that my actions could be affecting others.

After being in Oregon for a year, I had experienced a lot of personal growth, but I was getting restless. I thought about finding a good job and settling down in one place. I finished school with some college courses, but I dropped out before I could get my degree. I had been given money to finish school, however I began to use my school money for expenses and just to get by. I started to spend it on frivolous things just as Don said I would. I wanted to be carefree for a while.

Sara and I continued to see each other during the year and had little flings together, but I was too immature and irresponsible to let us become closer. We were honest with each other and started spending less time together as the year went on. I purchased an old car that needed some engine work, but I figured I could limp it around for a while. Driving Sara home from school, I was going too fast and blew the engine. Sara had enough of me and asked that we stop seeing each other. She broke down and saw me a few more times, but then our relationship ended.

About that time, I started hanging out with Randy, a friend who was studying to become a police officer. We would go to parties together and spent pretty much about all our time together now that I was not in school or working. My expense money was dwindling, and I decided to call my producer friend in Hollywood. I told him that I was on a break from school, and he was thrilled that I was in college. I figured that I was, in fact, on a break from school, so it didn't feel like I was lying to him. The producer told me that he had several muscle cars they were selling from a shoot that was finishing up. He said that if I wanted one, he would sell me one for $200. I did not hesitate and started on my way down to Los Angeles. The car was great and ran amazing. It was a two-door, baby blue, Ford Galaxy 500 with a supped up engine and a huge 4-speed shifter on the floor. That felt like the old me. The escapist; driving fast and living faster. I met a beautiful, voluptuous blond at a party, and we became quickly involved.

Joanne wanted to get a tattoo, and I told her I would take her and get one myself. On the way back from the tattoo parlor, she started play fighting with me as I was driving. One thing led to another, and we ended up kicking the shifter out of gear, and the car went into 1st gear at over 70 miles per hour. We heard a large bang, and I knew I had no gears left. I knew that there was no way I could afford a new transmission, so we just left the car sitting there and started hitching back home. The title had been signed over to me, however I never changed the plates from when it was in California. I called my mother for money to repair the car, but they felt that they had given me enough money and said no. I don't know whatever happened to the car, but I never saw or heard of it again. Joanne and I ended shortly after that, and I was on my way hitching back to Illinois.

Chapter 10
1980

I'd never forgiven Ken or Robert for taking advantage or trying to force themselves on me, but I fell back into old habits. I moved back in with Robert and started to drive more with Ken. One day, I pulled into a park in Palatine, Illinois and met Brenda. We got along so well, that we decided to move away together. We sold or gave away what little we had and moved to Tuscan, Arizona where I found a job as a cook up on top of Mount Lemmon, which was 28 miles up a mountain from Tucson.

I worked long hours, and still, we struggled to get by. When spring came, I was laid off, and they asked me if I could return the next season. Unfortunately, there was little work in the area, and we were forced to move back home. Brenda and I started selling drugs and partying constantly. We moved into the basement of my mother's house, and I contacted Robert to see if we could figure something out.

Robert and I would brainstorm ways to make it rich. Of course all the ideas we had were conceived through pot-induced thoughts. Robert had come up with the idea of selling cable decoder boxes that would unscramble subscription television stations. It was legal to build the boxes for yourself or sell the parts to make the boxes but not to build them and sell them completed. Brenda and I moved in with Robert, and we began our new business. The decoder boxes were easy to sell, and I even sold one to a policeman who lived in the area. Life seemed good at this time.

I had the business going with Robert, drove with Ken, and would occasionally visit my friends from Wayland Academy. One morning after partying all night with Alex from Wayland, we were driving back from Milwaukee when I passed out at the wheel. It had been snowing, and the car was spinning out of control in the middle of the interstate. Alex shook me awake, and I was able to veer off the road into a snow bank while holding Alex up against the seat. Alex looked at me in relief, just smiled and said, "I didn't know you cared." I knew it before, and I knew it then; I had a guardian angel. I had been in very bad places and very severe situations, but something always pulled me away in time. I believed it when things happened, but I didn't take that belief into my core.

While driving with Ken, I met Carlos, who was the same age as me, and we became pretty near inseparable. We would drive to Milwaukee almost every other weekend and visit the bar where Alex from Wayland was bartending, and we got to drink for free. We always seemed to have pot to smoke. Even though we partied and drank, neither one of us seemed to take it to excess. We took Carlos into the business we had started of building the ONTV boxes. Robert, Carlos, Brenda and I had a booming business with these boxes.

While stoned one night, I caught Robert in my bed again and threw him out. I told him that if he ever did it again, I would take whatever I had invested with him and leave. Not two weeks later, Robert tried again, and I took what I felt belonged to Brenda, Carlos and me and left. Robert, apparently, did not feel what I took was mine, and he called the police. One of the officers that arrested us was the one I had sold a box to when we first started. He told Brenda and me to bring in what we had taken. He said, "I'll give these back to Robert, and as long as he's not pressing charges, you are both free to go." He also advised us that several other agencies and a company for the subscription boxes had been cracking down on those selling the boxes, so he told us to lay low. Robert did not press charges, and that episode ended.

After buying a black 1967 Buick LaSabre, Carlos, Brenda and I headed out to Mount Lemmon, Arizona where I got a job as a kitchen manager. I was able to employ both Brenda and Carlos as my helpers. We kept on with our partying ways becoming even more reckless; driving down mountain roads while stoned, pulling donuts in the slippery, snowy roads and taking all forms of unnecessary risks.

At one point, I lost my car keys in the snow only to find them when things thawed. I was sure my guardian angel "took them away" from me, although I did not want to hear it and hotwired the car so that I could continue driving it.

My driving adventures continued. When I destroyed, or was lucky enough to successfully sell one car, I'd just buy another and start all over again. At one time, I owned a supped up Grand Torino, was driving though the curvy roads in the Ozarks, wasn't paying attention and by the time the tires were in the gravel it was too late and I lost control of the car. I knew enough to not hit the brakes, and after sliding down an embankment and just missing trees and other obstructions, I hit the gas and wheel hopped back out onto the road and continued on as if nothing had happened. There were other similar incidents. Driving without regard had become a challenge.

We were all laid off in the summer and took our time getting back to Chicago. When we got back to Crystal Lake, Brenda wanted to continue living the carefree life by dealing and partying, but that was taking its toll on me, and I refused. We parted ways in Chicago after being together for a year and a half and lost touch for quite a while.

Carlos and I hadn't seen each other for some time, and I heard he was living with a woman in Chicago that was dealing acid and other drugs. He showed up again sometime later wielding a baseball bat and demanding $200 from me. He said I owed him $200, and just in case I would not comply, he brought his brothers along for back-up. Carlos and I verbally went back and forth for a while because I did not remember owing him any money. I tried to confide in him, reminding him of all the things we had been through, all that had been exchanged between us and that even if I did owe him money this was certainly not the way to get it. Considering we had spent in the hundreds of

Memoirs of a Runaway

thousands together I just figured Carlos had lost it and I better just get him the money. His brothers did not seem to want to get involved in this matter and their facial expressions seemed to relay that to me. We had all liked each other, and they seemed as upset by this incident as I was. I ended up giving Carlos $200, and another friendship had ended for me. All the quick friends I made, all the things I had done to keep people around and get them to like me, all ended up for naught. It was a pattern though, one I hated, but yet was comfortable with.

With the summer of 1980 fast approaching, I wanted to go back to the simpler times in Arizona. I was always running away from or running to but never seemed to be able to settle down. When I got to Arizona, I was having an impossible time finding a job, any job. The places in Mount Lemmon would not be ready to hire me back until winter. I lived off of friends for the most part, but I wanted to be a responsible adult. I was a lost soul. I was looking for love, acceptance and any acknowledgement of self worth. I drove to waterfalls and hiked through the mountains just trying to find some sort of peace so that I might get to know my true self. I slept in my car as well as in shelters. Sometimes, I was able to beg enough money to eat, but I desperately wanted to work.

While hiking, I met a young woman who said that I could stay at her apartment while I got back on my feet. I was honest with her and told her that I was just looking to get on with my life. I told her that I didn't think it was a good idea for me to start a relationship and that I was afraid I would just end up hurting her like I had everyone else I had come into contact with. Unfortunately, she found the truth I had told her to be "charming." When some friends had come to pick me up and take me out for the day, I returned to her apartment to find my tires slashed and her hysterical with rage and jealously. She thought I had been out with another woman. I couldn't afford to fix the car, and I just left it there. I realized that I was leaving trails of women, cars and hurt people everywhere I went.

Arizona did not give me the same warm feeling I had remembered, and so I decided to hitchhike out to California. Again, I had to rely on churches and missionaries to keep warm, get some sleep and find food to eat. At one point, my mother wired me some money, but it did not last long.

When I reached San Diego, a bunch of bikers pulled up in front of me. I went up to them, unafraid of any danger that might be lurking. As I approached them, one of the bikers said, "Hey kid! Don't you know it is dangerous to hitchhike out here?"

"Ah, man. I'm glad you're here to protect me then," I replied. I began to think I was going to finally die when the bikers looked at each other and started laughing.

"Where are you going?" the biker asked.
"No clue," I answered.

"Well, jump on. We've been there several times, and we'll sure take you right to it," he responded.

I jumped on a bike driven by the gang's smallest biker. If I had to end up fighting someone, I wanted him to be the one. After driving for a while, we stopped to stretch our feet. One of the bikers asked me if I had ridden before, and I told him that I had ridden dirt bikes and bikes on ice in Crystal Lake. They gave me an old 67 Triumph Bonneville to ride, and we toured around for quite a bit. After a while, they had somewhere to go which clearly did not include me, but they told me to keep the bike and drove off. I drove around Orange County toward the beach. It occurred to me that the bike was probably hot and not registered, and I became nervous. I rode the bike for one last time along the beach, parked it, and walked away.

Chapter 11

1981

I was beginning to think that I might not become the success I always believed I would be. I had to call every friend and relative I had asking for money. At one point, I gave up and decided I didn't care if I starved to death, I would not call anyone else. That seemed to be what was going to happen. I was so desperate; I began hitchhiking back towards Illinois.

My appearance started becoming rougher looking, and I was feeling tougher inside. I was shutting down and closing myself off from the world. Once that happens, I think the world sees through this and notices that you need something but have nothing left to give. I could not recall the good times, the warm times or the carefree times in my life. The world became a cold and bitter place to me.

By the time I got to Nebraska, I was exhausted and stressed. I had been hitching for twelve days, and the only thing I had in my system was coffee and a ham sandwich that someone bought me. I thought about staying somewhere for a short time to get food stamps, but when you don't have a place to live and, thus, don't have an address, you aren't eligible, and so I continued on my way home.

Memoirs of a Runaway

A man named Joe picked me up and asked me if I wanted to get high. I told him yes but thought to myself that it would surely kill me. He pulled out what he described as "really good sensimilla." We stopped and smoked together and everything in my life seemed to become clearer. I knew that I had nowhere to go; I doubted I was wanted at home, and I had no future. This was it. I had hit bottom. I made small talk, but I kept these thoughts inside. Joe sensed my desperation and said, "Hey, if you'd like, I have pounds of this at home if you want to take some with you." Yet another person was giving me something for nothing. Of course I said yes, as I was a taker. I'd be able to sell it for food or use it for my own habit. We drove quite a distance before we reached his house. He was very generous and very kind. He drove me back to the freeway and asked me if I was going to be okay. I answered that I would be fine, and he dropped me off.

A few minutes after Joe dropped me off, it began to rain. Perfect, I thought. I wanted to suffer. I stood there for hours and was soaked to the bone. Finally, I decided to try to find someplace to get warm, but there were only a couple of gas stations in the area, and they were closed. There was a bridge a short distance away, and I decided to stay under it till the rain passed. I started to cry. I could not stop, and I could not regain control of myself. Every time I thought I might have hit bottom, I found a new level to sink to. I cried, and then I began praying. I gave the most heartfelt prayer I had ever said. I asked God to forgive me for what I was about to do, but I couldn't live anymore. It was too painful. I took a knife out of my bag and stabbed myself on the wrist. I started to pull on the blade to end my life…and I stopped. An overwhelming sensation came over me, a force that I had never felt before. I stood up and took a sock out of my backpack and wrapped it around my wrist. Newfound energy had surged through me, and I walked down to the road. I didn't even put my thumb out, and someone pulled over. This is a miracle, I thought to myself. The man who pulled over was in a Volkswagen station wagon, and he looked like the pictures and statues I had seen of Jesus. I jumped in his car. The first words he said to me were, "Have you confessed your sins to Jesus?"

I panicked a little and responded, "I went to church with my mom all growing up, and I know a little about the story of Jesus, but I don't know what to say."

"I can help you," he replied. He said the Lord's Prayer, and he asked me to pray and recite with him. "Say, Lord, I ask that you forgive me of my sins and come into my heart and be my lord and savior."

I bowed my head and peeked out of my eye to see if he was watching me. I recited that verse. He continued to talk to me, but I was feeling uncomfortable and staring at my wrist. I thought that God must have been looking after me. I didn't feel tired, or hungry, nor was I feeling the anxiety or the depression I had been feeling earlier. We did not ride a long way together, but I was realizing how rough of a night it had been. The sun was beginning to rise, and I still had not been to sleep. As he pulled off the interstate to drop me off, he said, "Do not worry; everything is going to be fine. You are going to be fine."

Memoirs of a Runaway

As I walked down the ramp, I was very concerned about getting a ride. I started to think about all that I had been through and what I must have put my family through. It seemed as if the walk down that ramp was the longest walk of my life. I was filled with thoughts and emotions I had never felt before. As I was about to slip into despair again, an elderly couple pulled over and asked if they could give me a ride. Of course I obliged and gave them my thanks. They made very little small talk and then said something that just floored me. The gentleman said, "Do you know how to live with Jesus in your life?"

I turned around and looked out the back window as if the last driver would be there making sure that these people continued his message. I replied, humbly, "I'm not sure." It had only been a few years that I had been out on my own, but it felt like a lifetime. I added, "I have lived so long like I have, I don't know if I know how to change."

The driver explained that Jesus died for us so that we may be forgiven and so that we could live an abundant life. I did know that, I'd heard the stories, but how did they know that I needed to hear that right then? As if in an epiphany, I realized that this was supposed to happen to me. I'd felt bits and pieces of this before, but this time I knew that God was really watching over me. Me. After what I've done, I wondered why He would even care at all about me.

The couple talked with me for quite a while and helped to put me at ease. I felt like everything they said was just for me, and I felt truly blessed. They went on to say that they had gone way past their exit but that they felt as if I needed them. They asked if they could give me some money, and I expressed gratitude to them and asked them to continue to pray for me.

They let me off at the next exit, and a van quickly pulled over and the driver said, "Come on in. Where are you headed?"

"Back to Illinois," I answered.

"Well, we're headed back home to Davenport, so we'll take you that far." There was religious music playing on the radio, and I heard Jesus' name in the lyrics. I actually felt nervous, like I could disappoint God by what I was going to do or say next. I knew that He was with me. I had felt it many times in the past, but I let the feelings pass quickly. God was not letting that happen this time.

The driver's wife continued, "We just got done with a gig and wanted to head back before we went out on the road again."

"Do you like Christian music?" another one of the riders asked.

"I don't know that I've heard a whole lot, but I like what's playing on the radio," I responded.

After a smile, the rider said, "That's us. We just recorded that, thank you."

"Wow, it sounds like the good old rock and roll I listen to all the time. I really like this." I remember talking for a little while longer, and my next memory was of waking up. "Man, I'm really sorry. I haven't slept in a really long time."

The four gentlemen and the one lady in the van looked at me with comforting eyes and sympathetic smiles. The woman asked, "You poor guy, when was the last time you ate?"

I couldn't even believe that she just asked me that. Why would she know or care? My eyes began to tear as I honestly could not remember. I told them what had happened, and I saw them looking at me with more concern than I ever remember from another human being. The moment I quit telling my story, the tone began to change as if they knew exactly what to say and do next. They looked at each other knowingly, and without a word, they pulled off the interstate and went right to a restaurant. One of the men sat down next to me and said, "We're going to take care of you, don't worry." I began to weep, and the woman took my hand and sat down beside me as well.

Without confiding in each other, they all began to talk to me about how much better my life would be if I lived with Christ in my life. I was overwhelmed and flattered that they took such an interest in me. I never had felt so much at peace and more comforted in my entire life.

They took me home with them, fed me again, and made sure I had a good night's sleep. The next day, they brought me to the Greyhound station where they bought my bus ticket and sent me home.

This time, I did not sit in the back of the bus or even considered partying. I thought about the pot that was still in my backpack that the guy in Nebraska gave me and wondered what I should do with it. I threw it in a garbage can in the bathroom and returned to my seat. I wasn't worried anymore. I started having conversations with

God in my mind. I promised him that his intervention would not be in vain and that I would make him proud.

I was so excited when I got home, I wanted to tell everyone. I told my brother, I told my mother, I told my friends. I know they were listening, but I was not sure anyone really heard, understood or believed me. I had conned so many people before, how could I blame them? But despite knowing that, I felt alone and depressed. The experience became a very personal one for me, and I did not share it with anyone else for a long time after that. I made a promise to God to pray to him everyday, and I kept that promise, though I always did so when I was alone. The shower was my time to give thanks to God or to ask for help.

For about eight months I lived with Mom and Don. I recuperated and tried to stay away from women and drugs. I knew I had heard the message, but I prayed I would be able to live it.

Chapter 12
1982

During the fall of 1982, I started driving a tractor-trailer again. For the first time, I was actually driving legally. I got my first chauffeur's license after having put on an estimated 250,000 miles driving tractor-trailers, motorcycles and even drag racing cars. I got a contracted job moving trailers from a warehouse in Schaumburg to a depot in Chicago. I would then unload the trailer onto six wheelers and do route sales. The money was very good, and I continued to try and straighten up and get my life in order. I believed that the trials were lessening, and I began to look at things in a different light. All of the trials I had gone through were just to teach me to be a better man. I refused to regret anything I had been through or resent anyone who had played any part in my life.

During a weekend in the summer of 1982, I went to a rock quarry in Wauconda, Illinois to go swimming. Always having been a sucker for a pretty face, I immediately was drawn to Renetta, one of the most beautiful women I had ever met. I tried desperately to get her to go on a date with me. Renetta was well read and well spoken, and I felt that she was perfect for me. I fell head over heels in love with Renetta, and, soon, I felt I couldn't be without her. We moved in together and got engaged. I tried to buy the condo where we lived because I knew it would make her happy. She left me feeling star struck and very insecure. I found myself doing anything I could think of to please her. Though I had no concrete reason, I was plagued with insecurity and felt that I could not trust her. Though I had not been particularly jealous before Renetta, I did not seem to be able to help myself when it came to her. When I came home from work one day, I found Renetta at our condo with another man. The man left quickly, and I told Renetta that I could not live with a woman that I could not trust. I broke up with her, but I was having problems being separated from her. I felt that I couldn't live without her. Though I had been sober for almost a year, I slipped back into smoking, drinking and partying. I tried to dull my pain, but even those vices did not seem to help.

In an altered state, I went back to the quarry where we had met. I opened up a bag of pills I had brought and started drinking them down with rum. After having found someone to love, despite all my progress, I was alone again. I don't know if it was the anxiety of the moment or God intervening, but I felt a rush of adrenaline as if I had just woken up…again. I got in my car and drove right onto someone's front lawn and screamed for them to call an ambulance. By the time the ambulance came, I had thrown up several times. They put me in critical care at the hospital, but the doctor later told me that because of all the rum I drank, I had thrown up most of the pills. The only thing I had succeeded in doing was raising my heart rate. They monitored me overnight and released me.

Over the next few years, I continued to drive a truck, straighten up and grew up a little at a time. I went back to Mount Lemmon and worked as a cook, kitchen manager and was even offered a partnership in the restaurant. I turned it down and told them that I did not feel responsible enough. I continued to drive a truck, also tried to get a job as a ski instructor, but it just happened to be a year where they got the least amount of snow they'd ever had.

Still in Mount Lemmon in 1983, I was offered an opportunity to stay at a beautiful cabin. The owner had rented out half of the cabin, and I was to be the roommate. My roommate never showed, and, luckily, the owner did not ask for more than the $500 a month rent.

That same year, my stepfather, Don, had been offered a job in Seoul, Korea at a power plant for Union Oil. My mom went with him and when Christmas came, I was alone. I had never missed a Christmas at home before, and it was discouraging that I could not go home that year. Sitting there in my loneliness, I heard a knock at the door. Two of the men I worked with were standing there telling me that I was not spending Christmas alone. I told them that I was fine, and they said, "You can either walk out of here with us or get dragged out, but no one should be alone on Christmas, so either way, you're coming with us." A lot of people from work were there, and it was very comforting to be with people who I knew cared about me. I knew that I would never forget their kindness.

Michael Kennon

In 1984, I moved to Kimberly City, Missouri to be with Grandma Dolly after my grandfather had passed away. I got a job again at Silver Dollar City as a ride operator. It seemed nice to be back to the simple life for a while. I always loved being in the Ozarks with friends and family, enjoying the beauty of the area. This time, though, I was able to fully enjoy it without partying. I was regular and dependable on my job, but I woke up one morning knowing that I did not want to go to work. A couple of hours later I heard my grandmother calling, "Michael, I need help." My heart just sank. My grandmother and I adored each other. She was a beautiful person, and I never heard her complain about anyone, or anyone complain about her. She never asked people for help; she was truly a giver and not a taker. I would have done anything to save her, but I could not. I ran to the neighbor next door, we called the ambulance and rushed her to the hospital.

When Uncle Gary arrived at the hospital, he yelled at me out of anger and said that I had killed her. My grandmother lived through the night, but my uncle would not allow me to go back in to see her. Gary felt that because I was around, it was too much for her heart.

I tried not to take it personally, because I knew how much he was hurting and how close he was to his mother. Grandma Dolly always expressed how happy she was to have me around, and I had been no trouble since I had returned, so I knew she loved having me around. She said that she had never been happier than with me living there the last few months. When Gary returned from the hospital, he kicked me out of her house. I was never even able to get pictures to take with me, only what I already had when I arrived.

Against my uncle's wishes, I stayed for the funeral. Grandma Dolly's neighbor, Tiny, sat next to me and said, "Michael, do you know how much she adored you? She would have wanted you to have the house."

I knew that was true, but I did not have the energy to fight with Uncle Gary. He was hurting, but I was also broken hearted. I listened as the pastor began to speak:

"We all knew Dolly. She was here with us every weekend, and I never remember her missing one of my sermons. We know that she is in a better place now with her beloved husband, Tony, which we all know is where she wanted to be." The pastor became teary, but continued his eulogy, "She would have wanted us to move on with our lives. She would have wanted us to be happy for her."

I had not known my grandmother went to church. She had been going for decades, and she never told me.

After Gary kicked me out, I had nowhere to go and no money saved. No matter what happened in my life, I always had Grandma Dolly, someone in the world who loved me unconditionally. Now that she was gone, and I was truly alone. I hit the road and went somewhere that I could ski all season and just lose myself. I landed in Flagstaff, Arizona working at a local bar called Dillon's where I did a little bit of everything.

I was soon on my way to Breckenridge, Colorado. I got a job driving a taxi, limo and shuttle and got a free ski pass. I started hanging out in a local bar and soon became involved with the wrong crowd. I began buying cocaine to use and to sell, and the dealer commented that I had bought $32,000 worth of cocaine in the last three weeks. He was impressed by that comment, but I started realizing that I would either end up getting caught, or very dead. I was also buying pot and acid to sell and sometimes used it myself. I was making $1,400 a week driving the cab but much more selling drugs. I was spending it all on booze, drugs and playing pool till all hours of the night. My cough was coming back, and I was sick most mornings. Until I took a shower and had my coffee, I could not breathe well, but still I kept on this destructive path. Always having been a pacifist, I began starting fights in the bar.

I knew that I needed to straighten up again, and I also knew that I was lucky not to be in jail, or worse. I would repeat to myself, "I'm better than this, I'm smarter than this." I stopped praying in gratitude or to ask for help. Instead I argued with God. I told him to change my addictions and habits. I could not understand why I kept ending up back in this type of lifestyle or why He allowed that to happen.

Since I was making so much money selling drugs, I quit driving the cab. One evening while I was having dinner and playing pool, a couple of guys asked me if I wanted to go out and get high. I went out with them, and one of them grabbed me from behind while the other searched me. I did not have a lot of pot on me, and they demanded I get them more. As I went to get my jacket, another man in the bar asked if I could get him some as well. I figured, why the hell not, I hate my life anyway.

Memoirs of a Runaway

So I drove out to Silverthorne, Colorado and got two bags of pot. As I hit the interstate, I saw red flashing lights everywhere as they pulled me over. They didn't even search me, but escorted me to a van where they promptly took me to a city building and put me in an interrogation room. I thought they had picked me up because I had two bags of pot and two grams of cocaine stashed away in my car in a scrunched up fast food take-out bag that I had thrown on the floor to make look like trash. I knew in the back of my mind since they hadn't arrested me yet, they were probably picking me up because the trailer next to the one I went in was making acid. Even when I had previously heard that, I choose to ignore it and pretended I had no clue what the officers were talking about. They asked very few questions and let me sit there alone under bright lights for what seemed like forever.

They would not allow me to make any phone calls and told me that I needed to go pack my things immediately and leave Summit County that night. If I were caught back in the county, they would arrest me. They said that they would be watching to make sure that I left, and they did. I didn't hesitate and got out of there as fast as I could.

I thought to myself; how can a man that has made a small fortune in a little over a year have absolutely nothing but a 1971 Chevy Malibu, some clothes, two bags of pot, two grams of coke and just a bunch of empty dreams to his name. I did not know where I was going or what I was going to do.

Ending up in a small café in Gunnison, Colorado, I sat alone in a booth for what seemed to be an eternity contemplating what I had again become, beating myself up for what a disappointment I had become to my family, friends, myself and God. I once gloated that I had gotten high and associated with many wealthy successful, influential people including many of my bosses, executives, lawyers, several policemen, an assistant district attorney, even a judge. Where are they now?

With no money, I thought that I would have to sell the drugs that I had with me in order to eat or go anywhere else. I was just tired. I no longer wanted those types of friends, I did not want those drugs in my car and I did not want to live like that anymore. I started asking God for help. I asked why he had forsaken me. I didn't feel that I deserved how I ended up. I was not out to hurt anyone. And I finally said, "Please, Lord, help me."

Chapter 13
1985

It was late in the year of 1985 when I turned 24; old enough to no longer be a runaway, but still running away. I was still talking to God, but I was demanding rather than asking. I was doing drugs again, and when the messages came that I needed to listen to, I often ignored them. Yet, the gifts kept coming. I was always comforted by the small voices I felt inside, but I would often refuse to listen. When I needed jobs, people would just offer them to me.

When I was sitting alone in the restaurant, I had struck up a conversation with an elderly gentleman. He told me that he had a ranch just outside of town and could use another hand. There was plenty of room at his place, and I was able to stay there too. So once again, I looked up to the heavens as Larry and I drove off to his ranch. It was a gorgeous piece of property. Larry was an independent, distilled water salesman. He liked the job, and, judging by the size of his property and his belongings, it appeared he did quite well. He had enough work on the ranch for me to be able to live rent free, and I was able to find construction work quickly and worked until the winter came.

When winter did arrive, I went to the Crested Butte Ski Resort to try to find employment. They were taking applications for just about every position there was. I wanted a good position where I could get a ski pass. I applied for the sous-chef position. They called me back twice, and I laid it on real thick. The interviewer said they had other applicants with better credentials, but they liked my enthusiasm and wanted to give me a chance. I wanted the position, although I had to tell them that I needed to take off for just a couple days to spend Christmas back in Illinois. My mom had decided not to spend another year in Seoul, so was just my brother and mom this time. I desperately wanted to see them for Christmas and told the manager that I would gladly work 135 hours every week, if I could just have off for that time. The manager hired me on the spot and reluctantly agreed to give me the time off.

It was Christmas 1985 when I went home to Crystal Lake to spend a few short days at home before I flew back to Gunnison. I settled right into the kitchen with my brother, Mark, and one of his friends. We had a few beers and I started telling them how long it had been since I had female companionship. Mark and his friend started mulling over names. There seemed to be a reason not to pick any of the names they recited until Mark's friend said, "Elizabeth, what about Elizabeth?" Mark laughed, and I had to ask what was wrong with Elizabeth.

"Well, I used to date her," replied Mark.

"Never mind then," I said. "I don't want to be with anyone you slept with."

"Actually, we never slept together, but she's...well, a bit enthusiastic."

Mark's friend agreed. "She's a bit on the wild side."

"So am I, call her up."

And they did. Elizabeth came right over, and I was pleased to see that she was a very pretty girl. She had blonde hair, blue eyes and an amazing body. All four of us started talking, and when Mark and his friend left, Elizabeth and I continued talking until 3 am. Elizabeth was very smart and had been working at McDonalds for a year. She'd saved up $2,600. It was a start, she said, of the money she would need to get out of Crystal Lake and be on her own. I told her about my job at Gunnison. When it came time to go back, though, I couldn't leave Elizabeth. We started talking about staying together, and I asked her to come back to Colorado with me. Elizabeth was excited about the prospect of leaving with me. She had lived a bit of the wild life herself and seemed ready, willing and anxious for a change.

We decided to tell her parents together. I thought it a good idea for them to meet me; so over we went. We shook hands and said our niceties. I told them about my job in Colorado. When Elizabeth mentioned her moving with me to Colorado, they didn't seem to react at all. What I hadn't given much credence to, was how old Elizabeth was. She was only 16, but her parents trusted her to make the decision. I didn't know if it was apathy or their blessing, but I chose to believe the latter.

Elizabeth and I flew back out to Gunnison a few weeks later. When we arrived at the ranch, we found my car buried under the snow. We also heard that Gunnison had been 40 degrees below zero for the previous two weeks. Neither Elizabeth, nor I, wanted to live in the freezing cold. The owners at my old job in Mt. Lemmon had once told me that my job was always available if I ever wanted to come back. Elizabeth agreed that we should give it a try. On the road, I called a friend to tell him that we were on our way. It was too late in the season to get my old job back on Mt. Lemmon, so we started talking about alternatives. We hooked up with my friend, and he told me that I would have a much easier time finding work in Phoenix. We hadn't settled in and figured we didn't have much to loose.

We found a small apartment by the university in Tempe. It was generally rented to college students who didn't have much to spend, but it was perfect for our price range. With that issue settled, I began looking for a job. I put in a few applications and noticed an ad for a local taxi company. The owner, Gary, interviewed me and asked me if I knew where the high rise hotel was. It was the only high-rise in the area, so I figured if I answered correctly, he was going to hire me. I told him the truth that I didn't know the area, but was good with directions. I knew I had a knack for survival, but this was a pivotal time in my life and it was very important to try and do the right thing and be honest. Gary said that if I could find the hotel, he could help me find anything else in the area, and he hired me.
Elizabeth and I were excited about getting started with our new life. I was driving the cab for 24 hours on and 24 hours off. The hours were long and Elizabeth was home alone for far too long. I loved driving the cab and got to know the area quite well. I also started making friends, but my life was centered on working and then returning home to Elizabeth. When I found out Elizabeth was

pregnant, I was thrilled. I had always wanted, and gave a lot of thought to, having a child, so I was immediately on board. The thought of having a child was transforming. Elizabeth also started changing quickly. At three months pregnant, her body was already changing, as was her whole outlook. She started becoming an overprotective mother. She wanted us to be perfect for this child. I understood the necessity of setting a good example, and I was trying to live as clean as I could. Elizabeth wanted me to stop smoking overnight, and I needed more time. I quit smoking inside of the house and around her, but it was going to take me a little while to stop altogether. Then it started becoming a battle of wills. I started resenting being given orders. The harder she pushed, the stronger I stood my ground. I spent my whole life running from people who tried to control my life, and then I was living with it again.

Part of the problem was that Elizabeth had nothing to concentrate on but her pregnancy...and me. She needed the support of family and friends and more attention than I could offer her. She never returned to work so that left her idle. The last thing I wanted to do was to move back to Crystal Lake, but Elizabeth wanted to. Even though I was angry about how she was treating me, I still wanted her to be my wife. If I wanted my marriage to work, we would have to move. Deciding that it was the right thing to do, we again prepared to relocate.

I was sure that the pregnancy was rough on Elizabeth, but it was brutal on me. Even after moving back to Illinois, she continued giving me ultimatums and threatening to end our relationship. It was a dual existence; growing resentment for Elizabeth and excitement over my impending fatherhood. As angry as I was, though, I still loved my wife. Every day that I saw her body change, I was more in love with her and the child I would come to meet.

When our daughter, Cassidy, was born, I was blinded by love. I've never experienced that kind of love before. Watching her birth was nothing short of a miracle, and that circle of love I felt for Cassidy wrapped around Elizabeth as well. Cassidy gave my life new meaning, and I immediately knew why I was on Earth and why I remained there despite everything I'd gone through. My purpose was to become a dad.

The next few years were the most precious and important ones to me that I had ever experienced. I had a child to raise. I worked hard, sometimes 14 hours a day. I worked a full-time job and then delivered pizzas at night. I wanted Cassidy to have everything in the world.

Despite my commitment to making my family work, Elizabeth was growing more distant. We fought like cats and dogs, and I could never remember about what, but the anger remained.

In 1988, I went back to driving a truck and hit the road as an independent operator. I went back to work with a local company, and we came up with the idea of running hotshot trucks. Hot shot trucks were named by farmers who put long trailers on the back of pick-up trucks to haul their hay, tractors and miscellaneous equipment. I named the business Kennon Transport and hauled conversion vans, cars and light freight.

It seemed that for every exciting step I took forward, there was always something negative weighing me down. Elizabeth and I were not getting along, but I was not going to leave my daughter.

The relationship got so tumultuous that I would fantasize about Elizabeth having an affair so she would be happier. It seemed that neither of us wanted the relationship to work. We had quit sleeping together for several months. Home alone one day, I started looking for something in the bedroom. I found letters from Elizabeth to other men. Perhaps that had added to the demise of our relationship, the fact that I thought she was having affairs. When I asked Elizabeth about the letters, she said that they were just "fantasy" letters and not to real people. The sad fact was that either way, I didn't really care. I wanted to be near my daughter, and I was willing to do just about anything to do that. Even though I'd always been a one-woman man, I did think about having an open relationship.

One night I was watching a movie with Mark and his friends at my mother's house. I started a conversation with one of the young ladies there, and we hit it off. It was exhilarating to have some female companionship after feeling so isolated from my wife. When we got hushed for the umpteenth time for talking through the movie, we went to my mother's room to talk in private. Suzanne started kissing me. I stopped her. As much as I wanted attention and passion, I just couldn't do it. I drove home after that, sat in my driveway and cried.

My life was my daughter and the road. It would come as a relief one day when I called Elizabeth from the road, and she told me that she wanted a divorce. I was not happy that she could not tell me in person, and I feared losing Cassidy, but I agreed.

With that decision behind us, Elizabeth and I were able to become friends again. We separated our belongings easily. Anything could be easily replaced, except for Cassidy, and that is where the trouble started.

Elizabeth was an awesome mother when it came to almost every area of Cassidy's life; it was me she didn't seem to like. We would rarely, if ever, agree on how to raise her. Elizabeth would yell at me in front of Cassidy, whether I was on the phone or in person. I could not bear to see my daughter's face when her mom and I argued in front of her. At first I started running away from my own daughter, but I knew that there was just no way that I could do that.

I tried going through the courts for custody rights, but that didn't help. They were in support of helping me see Cassidy, but it only got Elizabeth angrier.

For the next several years, I tried to see Cassidy as often as I could, but Elizabeth fought me all the way. I was only able to see Cassidy during my court appointed visits. I rarely, if ever, missed them. I wanted to know what was going on in her life, but it was difficult while only seeing her every other weekend.

While having Cassidy had given my life new meaning, my spirit was starting to break again. I tried to hold on as best I could. I mended my relationship with my mother and my uncle and began seeing other women, but I felt my heart start to harden.

Memoirs of a Runaway

I began to feel the way I had in the past when I'd turned to drugs and alcohol, but I didn't want to go back to that. But the void was there, and I started using women as my substance of the moment. I continued to drive a truck and tried to drive away from my feelings of emptiness, but it didn't work. I thought about just "dating" and staying away from any serious relationships. My main activity became soul searching. I had come so far, and still, I found myself lost. Thoughts of Cassidy learning who her father had been began to consume me.

My empty relationships with women continued, but I was working on healing every other relationship in my life.

I started learning things about my family that had been kept as family secrets. It was a shock for me to learn that my father had been married before, and I have two brothers from that marriage. Dad had left his first wife to start over, and no one spoke about it until I was twenty-three. One brother didn't learn about Mark and me until Dad died. I was happy to discover that one brother I contacted was very receptive, and we developed a close relationship.

I stopped to see Uncle Gary often when I was in Springfield, MO. My brother and I would often meet there. When we discovered that Uncle Gary had a brain tumor, we stopped by more regularly to take care of him. One day Gary told us, "Who would have thought it would be you guys by my bedside when I died." That was one of the last things I remembered about my uncle. He left me a little money, and my brother gave me a picture that Gary wanted me to have. I tried to pretend that a picture was good enough to replace a lifetime that was lost to partying and disrespect to those who loved me.

Negativity set in. It seemed as if everyone I had cared about had deserted me, including God.

I was told that my father had written thousands of articles and at least two novels, but I did not know where they were. My mother had a few clippings that were published in the newspaper, but I had nothing from him or from any of my relatives that were mine. As I became bitter, I wondered if I did have anything, would I even be responsible enough to keep them? Would I lose them? Would I respect the tokens, or would I just try to sell them?

I was getting done with a run and pulled into a truck stop in Detroit, Michigan to get some coffee and look for a reload. The waitress there was a pretty woman in her early 40's named Tina. Though I was twenty-eight, I was still shy around women. I did love to talk to people though, and we struck up a conversation. I finally had to say, "You're just too good looking to be in a place like this."

I blushed as the words came out of my mouth, but Tina answered, "Now, that was cute." She said that she was married but that her husband was gone a lot. She didn't need to work but wanted to get out of the house.

She admitted that she got hit on way too much but sometimes it was worth it. She was enjoying my company.

Again, the words escaped me before I could reel them in. "Do you want some company after work?"

"I think *you* want some company after I get off," she replied. I heard her make a comment about me just being another horny truck driver wanting to "get off." Jokingly, I assured her that I was and I did. The conversation stayed in the same vein until her shift was over. She came with me to my sleeper, which was a fancy walk-in with a refrigerator and a television.

It was there that we began what was probably one of the most erotic relationships I ever had. I continued to take runs back to Detroit and would see Tina frequently. Tina and her husband had not been getting along, although she was not hard-wired to be unfaithful. Once we started seeing each other, she told him. They separated, and we continued to see each other until she was to marry another man. We decided, at that point, that it was best not to see each other again. We didn't part sadly, and I knew we would hold fond memories of our time together.

In 1990, I started working with a trucking company that had a reputation for being one of the most elite carriers and being a very difficult company with which to gain employment. This company had some of the nicest trucks on the road. I stayed with them for about a year before buying another semi. I was working very hard, trying my best, and proud of what I was doing, but still not proud of whom I was. And one thing I knew I was, was lonely.

A friend convinced me to go out with him on a double date and we met at a bar in Crystal Lake. Paula was distant and told me that she was not interested in having a relationship other than friendship. This only seemed to spark my interest. I explained to her what I had been through and that the last thing I needed was to get involved as well. I told her that it was just refreshing to be with someone I didn't feel had a hidden agenda. Paula was genuine and easy to talk with. Paula had two children and expressed how nice it was to have adult conversation. I told her about the truck that I was driving at the time and mentioned that it was parked close by. We decided that it would be a quiet secluded place to talk and get to know each other, and since closing time was approaching, we decided to do just that.

Paula had lived with an alcoholic husband who was mentally abusive. She said that had become so comfortable and familiar to her, that she wasn't sure she'd know the difference between a healthy relationship and a bad one. Paula had done a good deal of soul-searching and self-help work. That would be a stepping-stone to my growth.

My progress had backtracked and taken a step or two backward for every step forward, but I felt that I needed to fix her. I was still not ready to deal with the issues in my life, so the repair job I wanted to do on her kept me free from analyzing my own demons.

Paula and I became best friends and disclosed everything to each other. I felt that I was falling in love with someone who was my best friend and my soul mate. I was sure that I could feel everything that Paula was feeling and understood her better than myself. I had never felt this way before. We became very close, moved in together and got engaged.

Situations starting arising which started fractures in my relationship with Paula. Alex from Wayland Academy came for a visit, and I caught him stealing from us to support his drug habit. I had to ask him to leave. A few months later, Tim, a friend I had from Crystal Lake, came for a visit when I was not at home. He told Paula that I had girlfriends all over, and he was sure I wouldn't mind if they slept together. When she declined, he told her that I had made a pass at his wife the last time I visited them.

I called Paula every night from the road. When I called this one night, she told me everything that Tim had said. She didn't believe him, but it hurt us both deeply. It had taken me a long time to build trust with Paula, and she continued to be guarded. This episode began to chip away at what we had developed. Our relationship was already a struggle, and we both suffered to make it work. It was even harder on Paula, as she had such a hard time trusting people. Most of Paula's family seemed to disapprove of me, and her children were always a challenge as I imagine most stepchildren could be when a new person comes into the picture. We loved each other, and we decided that moving to Oregon and starting over was the thing to do. I started talking to a limo company about driving for them in Ashland, Oregon. The owner told me that the business was for sale. He wanted a very small amount of money down, but mainly, he wanted someone to take over the payments for his business so he and his wife could semi-retire. I convinced him that I was his man.

Paula and I put the house up for sale and struggled to make it happen. We couldn't sell the house right away, but decided that I should go ahead and move out there, try to get everything tied down so that I did not lose that business opportunity and then send for her and the kids later. Paula agreed with me, although she cried for almost two weeks straight and must have felt that I was abandoning her. Things were never the same again.

When I arrived in Ashland, I did not have a place to live and no real capital. I was only able to get small jobs to survive on. I lost the limo company. I found a small place to rent until I could get back on my feet. I kept on with the constant contact to Paula, but things were going downhill fast. A couple of months went by, and she stopped taking my phone calls. All my letters were returned to me, unopened.

Lows kept coming not only because of my problems with Paula, but also because I had been fighting with Elizabeth over seeing Cassidy before I left. I hated putting Cassidy in the middle, but I just couldn't live without my daughter. Everything I owned had to be liquidated, including a baseball card collection I had since I was a child, so that I could get back to Illinois.

I started to wonder where God was in my life. Paula would not see me, I had no money, and I could hardly see the one person in my life who meant the most to me, my daughter. I figured that God must hate me to put an end to all my relationships. Maybe all the things I had done in my past would keep God from forgiving me. I even questioned the existence of God. My faith was being shaken, but yet something in me made me continue to pray. I scoured the bookstore for self-help books hoping to find the answers within their pages. It was obvious that I needed to make changes in my life, and while I had gotten away from drugs and alcohol, I had replaced them with unhealthy relationships. I was using women, sex and co-dependency to escape and fill the void in my life.

Memoirs of a Runaway

Eventually, I tried to test myself in the dating waters again. I put an ad in the single's section of the local paper. A beautiful young lady named Teresa answered my ad. She had three pretty daughters. Teresa was brutally honest, and we hit it off extremely well. It didn't take long for Teresa and me to move in together. For the next four years, we had a relationship that was passion driven. Money did not seem to be a problem for us, neither were her kids. The kinds of problems we started to have were over how much alcohol we drank and that fact that she did not believe in God. Even during my darkest times, I wanted to believe in God.

I prayed for an answer on what to do in this relationship. I had gotten involved in a direct marketing business and started working with Jim. We spent some time together and talked about everything. In the two weeks since we met, we covered about every subject we could think of. Then I said something not knowing how Jim would take it. "I'm having a hard time in my relationship because I really want spiritual growth in my life, and Teresa doesn't even believe in God." Jim's face lit up, and he smiled widely. He started quoting scriptures and seemed to be able to tell me what I needed to hear, not just what I wanted to hear. I asked him why he hadn't mentioned that he knew so much about the Bible, and he told me a story about when he first got saved. He was so excited about it and wanted to tell everyone. He felt then that he had become preachy and maybe even pushed people away. I remembered that happening to me when I had my experience many years ago. I wanted to tell everyone, but I was met with indifference, so I kept it to myself. Jim and I stayed friends even after I left that job.

I believed that most of my problems occurred because I had lapses in my belief. I did not know how I could grow with God in my life being with a woman who had no faith herself. Teresa and I had a good relationship for the most part. Neither of us wanted to get hurt again. So, we talked through our issues and even tried counseling. When it didn't seem to resolve our problems, I decided to move out. We stopped seeing each other, but ended on good terms.

Chapter 14
1996

In 1996, things seemed to be improving in most areas of my life. Cassidy was older, and I started seeing her more. I had healed a lot of my family relationships, and I had been away from drugs for many years.

Knowing that this was a crucial time in Cassidy's life and the fact that she had so much going on with school plays, soccer, band, choir, etc, I really wanted more time with her and started thinking about looking for local work.

It just so happened that one day while I was down in Atlanta delivering a load, I got a call from one of my shippers. Lisa called me from Chicago and asked, "Mike, can you pick something else up for me today?"

"I just picked up for you yesterday, Lisa", I replied sarcastically, "and am in Atlanta already today. I should become a trucking agent and start sending you trucks."

"When are you going to do that?" she asked enthusiastically.

"I don't know, I never really thought about it," I said, "I was just kidding." She went on to say, "I think you'd be great at that! I think you should look into it and I can offer you a lot of the business from here."

That day I began wondering why I hadn't thought of this before. I know the trucking business well and am compassionate with others and could do almost every facet of that business without even conferring with anyone else. I made a call to the carrier I was leased to at the moment and talked to the vice president. "Mike", he said, "I would love to see you as an agent for our company and you have our full support."

The wheels were turning now; I burned up a few calling cards and start talking to other people I had hauled freight for in the past. Almost all of them were not only receptive, but encouraging. How I am going to afford this, I thought. I have no real capitol and no business degrees. All I have are these 'life lessons'.

Feeling over-whelmed by the thought, scared to death to make another change and be stuck in an office, I called my direct-marketing friend to ask his advice. "Mike," he offered, "I am so confident you could be very successful at this, I'd be willing to loan you the money."

With that conversation in mind, the rest was history; Kennon Transport now became official from a driver to a trucking company. After I went home that trip, I began dispatching, hired a couple drivers to run the truck I still owned and even took a few more runs myself. I did not want to owe someone money, so was able to finance the office solely. After just a few months I could not even keep up with the amount of work I had and hired my brother, Mark, then over the next several years had at least 3 full time dispatchers.

I hadn't been ready to try a serious relationship again, but I was lonely for companionship. Back at Crystal Lake,

I went to a local festival with Mom, Mark and Cassidy. Mark and I chatted while Mom and Cassidy danced the day away. I looked around but told Mark, "It would be really hard to meet someone here with this many people around." A couple of women sitting across from us had been listening in. When there was a lull in the conversation, one of the women got my attention and motioned to her friend and said, "Well, she's single."

The young woman she pointed out was named Sue. After both of us blushing and then recovering, we started to talk. Sue may not have had as many hard experiences as I had, but she had a hardened heart from painful relationships in her past. I figured we made a good couple, but I hoped it wouldn't go the way that things had with Teresa and me. Sue had shut herself off a bit from the world and didn't want to trust or confide in others. I had finally learned that I did not want to get involved with someone unless I could communicate well with her.

As Sue and I continued to date, we began to share each other's secrets and build trust ever so slowly. We were developing a relationship, but we were apprehensive. I knew that Sue deserved to be happy, but she held onto her resentments from the past.

We were at a roadblock. I had hoped we could go further, but Sue told me she would have a hard time communicating with me the way I wanted. We still had feelings for each other, but we did not want to become casualties of yet another failed relationship. We parted as friends, and as time passed, I started dating again. Even though we'd put the romantic relationship on hold, I could not get her out of my mind or out of my heart. Sue had amazing qualities, and I knew that she was just being honest with me. She did care for me, but she didn't want to hurt me. Whenever I needed someone to talk to, Sue was always there for me, but I felt it was more than as a friend. We took a chance and started dating again.

As time went on, Sue remained by my side. She was very good to me, good to my daughter and remained faithful, honest and open. She didn't do those things to make me happy, it was just who she was. She also gave me the time and space to discover who I was. We did not need to fix each other, just to be there to support each other as we worked on ourselves.

Sue and I remained a couple, and on our sixth anniversary of being together, I woke one morning to find her staring at me.

"What?" I asked alarmed.

Sue smiled and asked, "Will you marry me?"

I laughed and looked at her again. "You're serious?"

"I'm tired of waiting for you to ask," she replied.

She was gracious and gave me time to think about it before I responded. I knew I loved her and she in return, loved me. I had many relationships, but I did not want another failed marriage. Sue was a different person though. We were not being young and impetuous. We had been together for six years and each had encouraged the other to grow. I did not want to let anyone else down or have myself let down again.

I realized that it took me awhile to accept or receive gifts because I did not feel worthy. Once I said, "Yes, I will marry you" to Sue, I committed myself completely to her and our relationship. Sue and I married in July of 2002 on one of the most beautiful days I'd ever seen. The ceremony took place along the Rock River in Oregon, Illinois. The pastor who married us was the same one who had married Elizabeth and me. He also performed marriages for both my mom and my brother. We had our reception on a paddle wheel boat with about 80 people. I knew I had been given a gift in this woman, and although I'd not danced more then a dozen times in my life, I danced the entire day. Though Cassidy was becoming defiant at this point, she did come to the wedding. We were grateful and had a wonderful time with her. As we were docking, the captain came over to me and said, "This has been such a good crowd, it's such a beautiful day and everyone's having so much fun, we're going to let you have the boat for another hour if you'd like." It should have cost another $200 for the extra hour, but he didn't charge us. That felt like another good omen that this union was meant to be.

Things were great at the wedding, although Cassidy was becoming a challenge. She had been busy at school and doing more things with her friends, so we had not been spending a lot of time with her. Maybe it was being a teenager, but she started saying hurtful things to me. We continuing to make an effort to be part of her life, but she was making it obvious she did not want to be part of ours.

After a year of Cassidy not staying with us and only seeing her a couple of times during the previous year, Sue and I started talking about moving somewhere warmer. Because the trucking business could be done over the phone, we could live anywhere. We put the house up for sale at a price over the appraised value, and we got a

Michael Kennon

buyer within two weeks. Business was good, and we could only take off a week to look for a new home. We decided on Charleston, South Carolina since it had been one of my favorite places when I drove a truck. Luckily, we found a home quickly and began planning our move.

We had little or no debt when we decided to move, but we put $3,600 on our credit card for the moving company. It was November when we decided to move, a slow time for the business, but we knew things would pick up again in a few months. We continued to charge things knowing we would pay it all off by the summer. By July, business had still not picked up the way it should have. Before we knew it, there was another $16,000 worth of credit card debt, and although the business could pay for itself, it was not paying our living expenses. Sue and I were getting desperate and started looking for extra jobs. I was offered a job with a decent salary, benefits and a company car, but I would have to leave my job. This was my worst dilemma and my biggest nightmare. I couldn't take the job right away, and I told the owner I would need time to think about it. He agreed. Sue and I became distraught. We wanted to grow our own business—it was a dream of ours, but we also needed to pay our bills.

Sue and I started going to some churches in the area looking for help, but things kept getting worse for us.

By late July into early August, it got extremely hot, and our air conditioning system went out. We got quotes of $12,000 to fix it. We turned in a claim to the insurance company, but they told us that the system was too old and had not been properly maintained. Then we found pinhole leaks in the copper pipes of our house. The pipes had been leaking down the walls, growing mold, and Sue and I were getting sick from it. Quotes on replacing the copper pipes and those repairs were coming in at over $20,000.

Even though Cassidy wanted little involvement in my life, she started calling me and accusing me of not taking more responsibility. She was bitter because she felt I should be paying more child support and that I should be paying for her college also. I was paying support as well as sending extra money, but that didn't seem to matter to her.

Sue and I were at our wits ends. We came into this marriage with issues we both had to deal with from our pasts. Sue's issues with abandonment, for which she still harbored bitterness and resentment, and my many issues that I had still to deal with. We already had our work cut out for us without all these new problems that were being heaped upon us.

One thing Sue and I planned on doing was finding a way to grow spiritually. There were times that I resented God and wondered whether he even existed, but something always pulled me out of the darkest times of my life. Still, nothing was working. We kept a pretty good attitude about all of this, but we knew we were going to need help, serious help.

Chapter 15

2003

I had always been aware of the story of Jesus. I loved the stories and the affirmations in the Bible. To me, everything I had gone through had included God. Whether I was asking for help or arguing, apologizing, or wondering where he was and if he existed.

Sue and I were out of ideas. There was one church we went to that we liked, and we decided that we were just going to turn our lives over to God and dedicate our efforts to Him.

I had always wanted to grow spiritually but was also terrified of doing so. I thought that if I lived the way that God intended, I would have to give up all the things I enjoyed, or that I would not be capable of living the way he would want me to. I started thinking, okay, if I were a father (which I am), and my son or daughter came to me after all I'd done and asked for forgiveness, would I? I figured that I would, and so, perhaps, there was hope for me.

Sue and I went to a couple of services on Sunday. The church we found was a Bible-based church that promoted working in small groups and finding your gifts. They worshiped first, usually did a drama skit, and then maybe showed a movie clip and did a sermon. The church was interdenominational and seemed to find ways to relate to just about anyone. They said their philosophy was simply to help everyone find a way to interpret the Bible and to teach us to relate the stories in the Bible to our everyday lives so that we could understand and apply them where necessary.

We went to their introduction to the church meeting to learn more about their philosophy. We attended their new members' classes and got baptized.

When Sue and I were in the new members' classes, they started explaining tithing. This was a real challenge for us. Giving up 10% to the church meant giving up 10% of something we didn't have. We learned that in the Bible, this was the only area that says to "test" God. If we gave to Him, He would pour out His blessings to us.

When Sue and I were done with our new members group and got baptized, we went to and started several small groups including Alpha course, Purpose Driven Life, 40 Days of Community, Passion of the Christ and others, and continued to go to service every Sunday. We began watching Joel Osteen, listening to Joyce Myer and started listening to Christian music in our house and in the car.

Toward the end of August, we were $23,000 in debt on our credit cards alone. Sue and I agreed to take our leap of faith even further. We remained committed to our church and starting tithing 10% of our income for the first time. One of our neighbors, whose wife recommended the church, had come over to look at our heating and air system. He was a foreman for a heating and air company and said he wanted to help. He did the whole job with warranty for $3,000. Then I had lunch with a friend who lives in the area and owns a home improvement business. As soon as I told him we found mold growing in the house, he said, "you can't live with that," and that he would have his crew over at 6 am the next morning. He said he would also attempt to turn this all into our insurance company and the next day began the work. He said he would complete the work and, if necessary, we could make payments. During the construction, there was even more damage then we had originally thought, but we kept our faith. Another friend, who was a plumber, came and did all the plumbing work on the entire house for us, and although he said he'd do it for free, we wanted to pay him. It still ended up being far less then we would have paid.

The insurance company denied the claim to replace faulty equipment and parts, but they did agree to pay for all the damages. We ended up getting a check from our insurance company that not only paid for the original work but for the additional damage we found along the way.

Almost immediately, a huge job came in that paid most all of our bills. It was a hard time for the trucking industry because of the rising costs of fuel and insurance. Many companies were struggling at a time when we got extremely busy. Work seemed to come from everywhere all the way through the slow season. By April, we made enough to pay all our bills, pay our current living expenses and put $10,000 in the bank.

In the three years that followed, business had not slowed down for us. We even complained, jokingly, that there wasn't enough time for a vacation. We knew that it was a God thing that helped us with everything we went through—individually, and as a couple.

In late 2006, Sue and I thought about selling our house, paying off the rest of any debt we had and looking for a home that better suited us. We wanted to start taking the necessary steps to make investments towards our future. Sue saw a house on the water and said, "I know it's out of our price range, but let's go look at it." We fell in love with the house and the area. We put a bid in for $15,000 less than the already marked down asking price. The sellers accepted. Then the house appraised for $30,000 more then we paid

My daughter, Cassidy, and I had started talking again. Sue and I picked her up when she flew down from Chicago to come stay with us a while. We continued to live our lives and include Cassidy in our endeavors. We took her to church and to see Joel Osteen. This was one of the biggest miracles and the most important of all the blessings we were beginning to receive, as Cassidy seemed eager to be a part of our new lives. During one of the sermons, Cassidy told me how well she could relate and enjoyed the message.

Sue and I were beside ourselves with everything changing in our lives and all the blessings pouring in. Sue and I made that whole experience our testimony and knew that we would praise God whether things were good or bad. God is in control, not us, and that was okay. I had learned my lesson, and I knew what life was about for the first time. It was never about me. It is about God.

Conclusion

Nothing came as an epiphany for me, it was a process. I wished I was one of those people who went through an eye opening, life changing, born again transformation, but even when God spoke to me, I had not been ready to receive His wisdom. Perhaps some of the things I went through would have affected other people quicker, but I guess I'm just a little slow sometimes. Or as Cassidy says, "What's wrong with you guys?" or her other variant, "boys are dumb."

Looking back, it seems that there might have been an opportunity, a person or a "door" that was put in front of me almost every time I asked Him for help, but I was too stubborn to pay attention or make the right choices.

Grandma Dolly was surely one of my guardian angels, or maybe her constant praying for my safety, wellbeing and success kept pulling me back on track, even when I strayed from it. She was steadfast in her belief, and so she may have had some pull with those in high places, namely, God.

I remember the conversation I had with Jim from the direct marketing job. When Jim wanted to tell everyone about his being saved, people were put off by it. I felt the same way. When I was in desperation and felt like a miracle happened in my life, I was bursting to share my experience, but either no one believed me, or it wasn't something they were ready to hear for themselves. I learned to make Jesus a very personal thing and have kept Him to myself ever since.

I've heard the phrase, 'His way', but never really got it. Until I learned that it was never just 'about me' it was about putting my faith where it belonged and my purpose will be revealed to me! Suddenly I realize what it all means. It's not about the rules, it's about a relationship. I do have a purpose, and He is my creator, not the other way around. It never worked 'my way'.

I heard a pastor put it this way: 'The Bible was written 2,000 years ago and is the only book that has not been rewritten; not a paragraph, not a coma, not a period has been added or changed.' So why would I question the Bible? The Bible is about love, grace and integrity. Why would I argue that? People don't go up to an inventor and tell them how their invention works. People have faith in the inventor because the inventor knows how it works! I believe the Bible is a manual written by our creator.

Even if I continue to question Him, I know how things are going to be now. I know that if God closes a door, it will be because there's something else better at the next door or He was protecting me. I cannot wait to see what He has in mind for us next; I look forward to it and am filled with anticipation.

I think of the experiences I've been through and now can see them as lessons I have learned, and I have no regrets. I believe that Jesus was God's gift to me, and anyone who chooses to receive Him can and will.

This story is not over, it's only beginning. I am no longer running away from something. I'm running to it. I am not lost, I am found. And with God's will, I will continue to enjoy the life He intended for me. I now realize that it is faith that gets us through, and His grace that shows us the way. I believe God gave us free will and that whatever we run away from will only find us and become a part of us. It's all about the journey—how to accept it and the choices we make. I truly believe that nothing is impossible with God and choose to run to Him.

Some people are lucky to find love once in their lives. I believe God has given me the gift to love here on earth. He has also granted me the opportunity to have a personal relationship with His son, to be loved forever and to have everlasting life. If I'm right, I'm going to heaven and might have some supernatural intervention here on Earth. But what if I hadn't made this choice and there is a God? Hell does not sound like a place I want to be or a place I want to return to.

As for my past, even though He may not have liked what I had to say or do, He loves that I said it to Him. Another way I look at it is that God is eternity, so that makes us very young. If a one-year-old spilled something, the parent is not going to disown them or even judge them; the love will be the same. He was always there in my life, even when I didn't believe. The Bible says if I ask for His forgiveness, He will forgive me and forget what I did. That's a two way street, though. We also need to forgive those we feel have wronged us. I tell my story through a child's memory. How I saw things as a boy would differ from how I would interpret them as an adult. Now, I can ask for explanations if I feel I need them. And whether the explanations or apologies make sense or whether the puzzle pieces fit where I need them to, either way, I can forgive and be forgiven. One of the greatest gifts we can give ourselves is asking for His mercy; He knows what we're going through and what we've been through, and if we forgive others and forgive ourselves, we can free ourselves from the pain of the past occurrences.

I now know that God has never left me…I left Him. I hear a different voice in my head now. Instead of asking myself more questions and arguing with Him, I submit myself to Him and confess my secrets. Now I hear, "You are welcome."

All that I am receiving now are His blessings. I understand what "in God We Trust" means. I describe my life now like I'm in the 4th grade, but in God's school; a child of His, an enthusiastic, overjoyed, fun filled youth with all his innocence and life ahead of him.

I am hopeful that my story can help others—that I can share my beliefs where they will do good. My niece was struggling like I was. Sue and I spoke to her about the fact that we truly believed that everything had changed since we devoted our lives to Christ. I knew we had planted a seed when she entered a rehab facility and started writing letters of apology toward the people she had offended and hurt. We had inspired her, but it inspired me more. There are so many impressionable kids out there, and it is up to all of us to help them and their parents.

I am open to all kinds of experiences in this world. When I started getting an aching feeling to get my thoughts down so that perhaps I could help someone else, I put it off for a while. Then the dreams came, and the urgent feeling that it was something I needed to do. I see myself one day working my trucking business on the road while I talk about my experiences to others in need so that I may help them and give them support. And so with that, here is my story. God's story. And you are not alone.

The End

End Notes:

I have a very deep and loving relationship with my mother and she has been the one constant in my life. I know there were times she may have mentioned that she would rather have had begonias than children, but I was extremely difficult to deal with and put her through hell, repeatedly. While I may have felt that she married my stepfather and stayed with him for monetary reasons, she feels differently. As my father left her the house, and she had her own investments, she denies that was her motive. She feels that my stepfather was never abusive in front of her, and if he was, she intervened. She also states that she never knew she had a temper until dealing with Don's step-parenting techniques. One Christmas her gift request was that he treat her sons well.

Mom also felt that Don treated my brother, Mark, as poorly as he did me.

She does admit that she was extremely permissive with me, but she also forgave me over and over again.

I love you, Mom. God Bless.

Michael Kennon

Runaway Statistics and Resources

According to Runawayteens.org and 1800runaway.org, "one in seven kids between the ages of 10 and 18 will run away at some point. And there are 1 million to 3 million runaway and homeless kids living on the streets in the United States."

Motivations for running away

"47% of runaway/homeless youth's indicated that conflict between them and their parent or guardian was a major problem.

Over 50% of youth in shelters and on the streets reported that their parents either told them to leave or knew they were leaving but did not care.

80% of runaway and homeless girls reported having been sexually or physically abused. 34% of runaway youth (girls and boys) reported sexual abuse before leaving home and forty-three percent of runaway youth (girls and boys) reported physical abuse before leaving home.

Childhood abuse increases youths' risk for later victimization on the street. Physical abuse is associated with elevated risk of assaults for runaway and homeless youth, while sexual abuse is associated with higher risk of rape for runaway and homeless youth.

Memoirs of a Runaway

Risk factors associated with running away

Over 70% of runaway and throwaway youth in 2002 were estimated to be endangered, based on 17 indicators of harm or potential risk. The most common endangerment component was physical or sexual abuse at home or fear of abuse upon return. The second most common endangerment component was the youth's substance dependency.

12% of runaway and homeless youth spent at least one night outside, in a park, on the street, under a bridge or overhang, or on a rooftop.

7% of youth in runaway and homeless youth shelters and 14% of youth on the street had traded sex for money, food, shelter, or drugs in the last twelve months when surveyed in 1995.

32% of runaway and homeless youth have attempted suicide at some point in their lives.

Approximately 48.2% of youth living on the street and 33.2% of youth living in a shelter reported having been pregnant.

50% of homeless youth age 16 or older reported having dropped out of school, having been expelled, or having been suspended.

Demographics of runaways

Michael Kennon

Runaway youth are 50% male and 50% female, although females are more likely to seek help through shelters and hotlines.

*40% of youth in shelters and on the street have come from families that received public assistance or lived in publicly assisted housing. * As indicated to shelter staff at a federally funded runaway or homeless shelter"*

Contact Phone Numbers:

http://www.runawayteens.org/
Contact number 786-317-8774
TOLL FREE
http://www.1800runaway.org
Call 1-800-RUNAWAY

INTERNATIONAL
"Just Say No" International - Drug & Alcohol Help
800-258-2766 (24 hrs)

CANADA
Kid's Help Phone 1-800-668-6868 (24 hrs)
AIDS/Sexually Transmitted Diseases Info 1-800-772-2437
End Abuse - Domestic Assault Line
1-800-END-ABUSE (24 hrs)
Zenith Child Abuse Reporting & Help Dial the Operator
and ask for "Zenith 1234" (24 hrs) USA
Eating Disorders Help Line 1-800-382-2832 (24 hrs)
Domestic Abuse/Assault 1-800-333-SAFE (24 hrs)
Teen AIDS Line 800-234-TEEN (Mon-Fri)
800-440-TEEN (weekends)

National AIDS Line 1- 800-342-AIDS
National Teen Gay & Lesbian Hotline 1-800-347-TEEN
(Thurs.-Sun., 7 pm-11:45 pm ET)
Family/Children's Mental Health Hot Line
1-800-654-1247 (24 hrs)
National STD Hotline 1-800-227-8922 (24 hrs)
Child help USA - Child Abuse Reporting 1-800/4-A-CHILD
(24 hrs)
Family Violence Help Line 1-800/222-2000 (24 hrs)
National Runaway Hot Line 1-800-HIT-HOME (24 hrs)
Runaway Help Line 1-800-621-4000 (24 hrs)
Covenant House Crisis Support 1-800-999-9999 (24 hrs)
Suicide Help Line 1-800-SUICIDE (1-800-784-2433)
Youth Crisis Line 1-800-448-4663
RAINN - Rape Support Line 1-800-656-HOPE
Pregnancy Support and Advice 1-888-4-OPTIONS
General Crisis Counseling 1-800-785-8111

The resources and information given, such as statistics, phone numbers, web sites, and organizations, were the result of a search done on the World Wide Web and may or may not be accessible or accurate today. Other permanent solutions, such as talking to a Bible based church pastor or associate, private organizations, government, municipal or local agencies may be available.

[1] *"RunawayTeens.org,"* http://www.runawayteens.org/, *accessed January 17, 2008, pages 125-128.*

[2] *"National Runaway Switchboard,"* http://www.1800runaway.org/, *accessed January 17, 2008, pages 125-128.*

Memoirs of a Runaway

contact the author and check for
additional projects through this site;
http://www.memoirsofarunaway.com

Michael Kennon

Memoirs of a Runaway

Michael Kennon

Made in the USA
Charleston, SC
09 September 2013